CAMBRIDGE SKILLS FOR FLUENCY
Series Editor: Adrian Doff

Listening 3

Joanne Collie
Stephen Slater

Published by the Press Syndicate of the University of Cambridge
The Pitt Building, Trumpington Street, Cambridge CB2 1RP
40 West 20th Street, New York, NY 10011–4211, USA
10 Stamford Road, Oakleigh, Melbourne 3166, Australia

First published 1993

Printed in Great Britain
by Scotprint Ltd, Musselburgh, Scotland

ISBN 0 521 36749 2 Book
ISBN 0 521 36546 5 Set of two cassettes

GO

Contents

Thanks

The authors would like to thank the following people for their help with the recordings: Malgorzata Serwan and Shirley Slater (Unit 8A); members of the Oxford Caving Club (Unit 14A); Frank Packenham (Unit 14B); Winston Head, Doreen Kartinyeri, Leila Rankine and the Museum of South Australia (Unit 20).

The authors and publishers would like to thank the following people for their constructive suggestions on the pilot material without which the improvements to the book would not have been made: Dominic Fisher, Filton College, Bristol; Sean Power, ASC Language Training, Geneva; Tony Robinson, Eurocentre, Cambridge; Christine Vasey, English Language Unit, University of Liverpool; Sue Hancock.

Map of the book

Unit	*Functional areas*	*Vocabulary areas*	*Listening strategies/ activities*
1 **Jobs, desirable and undesirable**	Discussing; giving reasons; assessing qualities.	Occupations; personal qualities.	Listening for specific information; predicting; matching with a summary.
2 **A bit of a nightmare**	Describing and explaining.	Dreams, bad dreams; causes.	Listening and completing; predicting and matching; note-taking.
3 **Puzzles**	Describing; deducing; solving.	Games, puzzles; puzzle clues.	Listening and matching; listening for clues and checking answers.
4 **How do you . . . ?**	Describing regular activities; discussing.	Shopping; journeys.	Listening and evaluating; completing a flowchart; matching.
5 **National anthems**	Describing; offering viewpoints.	National anthems; national pride.	Matching; comparing; note-taking; rating.
6 **Crime and punishment**	Describing; reporting.	Crime; punishment.	Listening for detail; note-taking; comparing.
7 **Memorable parties**	Giving opinions; narrating.	Parties; social conventions.	Listening for particular information; guessing; answering questions.
8 **Babies, brothers and sisters**	Interviewing; narrating; remembering childhood.	Babies; hospitals; siblings.	Confirming guesses; listening for interesting information; matching.
9 **Brief encounters**	Recounting meetings; conversation 'filling'.	Reactions; physical features.	Listening and note-taking; listening for 'fillers'; judging attitude.
10 **The hole**	Story reading; reacting to a story.	Towns; bridges.	Predicting; guessing; comparing with own reactions; following a story.

Unit	*Functional areas*	*Vocabulary areas*	*Listening strategies/ activities*
11 Teeth and dentists	Recounting experiences; narrating.	Teeth; dentists; dental treatment.	Listening for detail; evaluating experiences; matching with own experience.
12 Take our advice	Giving advice; describing visuals.	Driving; business.	Predicting; labelling; assessing importance of advice.
13 Emotions	Describing emotions.	Crying; anger.	Matching; answering questions; comparing.
14 Flirting with danger	Discussing experiences; giving views.	Caving; gliding.	Matching with visuals; completing notes.
15 Feet and walking	Describing; narrating.	Feet; walking.	Noting important words; checking; following a story.
16 Credit cards	Describing uses; narrating.	Credit cards; social values.	Listening for specific information; following the order of events.
17 Friends and friendship	Defining; explaining.	Friendship; friends.	Listening for key information; finding reasons; listening for pleasure.
18 Learning languages	Talking about the past; describing stereotypes; giving reasons.	Languages; learning languages.	Matching; listening for detail; note-taking.
19 A multicultural world	Discussing relationships.	Marriage; family; relatives.	Making notes; extracting main issues; listening.
20 Ngarrindjeri	Talking about your past and your people; reciting a poem.	Australian Aborigines.	Listening for specific details; following the logic of a story; listening for enjoyment.

1 Jobs, desirable and undesirable

A Jobs: My idea of hell, my idea of heaven

1 If you were unemployed and couldn't find a job in your own profession, would you take a job in:

	Yes	*No*	*Maybe (it would depend on . . .?)*
an abattoir			
an AIDS clinic			
a nuclear power station			
a casino			
a factory			

See if your answers are the same as the student next to you, and if you answered 'maybe', say what it would depend on.

Can you name a minimum salary that would persuade you to change your mind about those jobs which you said you wouldn't take?

2 Listen to three people describing the jobs they would hate to do. As you listen, tick the jobs that are mentioned in Exercise 1. How many of these were reasons given for not wanting to do the jobs?

a) It would drive me mad.

b) It would be too much responsibility for me.

c) It would be so boring.

d) It would be like a form of torture.

e) I would be incapable of doing it.

f) It would be too repetitive.

Which speakers give which reasons? Listen again and check your answers with another student.

What are your own feelings about the jobs discussed? What other jobs would you really hate to do and why?

3 What would be your ideal job? Discuss your answer to this question with other students and give an explanation for your choice.

Now listen to the same three people describing the jobs they would really like to have. As you listen, complete the table:

	Jobs mentioned	*Reasons given for choosing them*
Speaker 1	archaeologist	
Speaker 2		best baseball team in the world
Speaker 3		

Did they mention any of the jobs that you chose? Did they have similar reasons for choosing them?

4 **Extension** What are the most important aspects of job satisfaction as far as you are concerned? Compare ideas.

B Have you got what it takes to be a . . .?

1 This person used to be called an air hostess or stewardess. Now she's often called a flight attendant. Which of the following is the most likely reason?

a) There has been a change in fashion.
b) Flight attendant is a better description of the work she does.
c) Flight attendant can be used for both men and women.

Jot down some personal and physical qualities that a person needs for this job. Compare and discuss your ideas with others.

2 Listen to a woman talking about the time when she wanted to be an 'air hostess'. What qualities does she mention? Note down any that are not on your lists.

Do you think the situation she describes has changed?

3 What job is suggested here?

What sort of personality characteristics do you think are most important for this job? Mark three of the following (using 1 for the most important, then 2 and 3):

decisive stable sympathetic friendly independent

emotional brave authoritative strong empathetic

self-disciplined

Compare your choices.

4 You are going to hear someone talking about a friend who was unable to cope with this type of nursing. Here are three possible summaries of what happened:

a) She didn't care enough about her patients to do the job well.
b) She couldn't separate her own feelings from those of her patients, and became mentally ill herself.
c) She couldn't adapt to working in an institution and stopped doing it properly.

Listen and choose the summary that is closest to what happened.

5 **Extension** If you were an official in the hospital where this person worked and she had asked you for a reference for a job of a totally different kind, would you mention the difficulties she had had as a nurse or would you only talk about the positive qualities she possessed, that were relevant to the job she was seeking?

2 | A bit of a nightmare

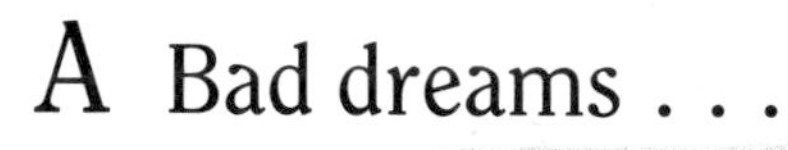

A Bad dreams . . .

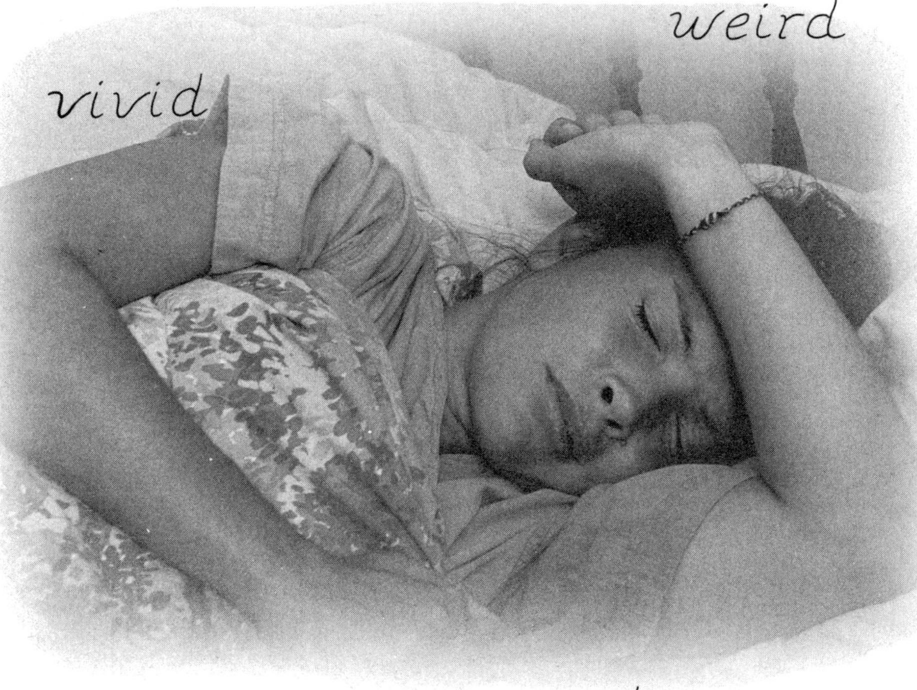

1 What adjectives do you associate with the expression 'bad dreams'? Add some words to the picture.

2 Have you ever had any dreams which involved:

being chased? ☐ being attacked? ☐ being trapped? ☐

falling into a deep hole? ☐ being lost in a strange place? ☐

being paralysed? ☐

Describe one of your dreams to some other students. Has anyone else in the class had a similar dream?

3 You are going to listen to two people describing their bad dreams. Choose one of these pictures and try to imagine the bad part of the dream. Exchange ideas.

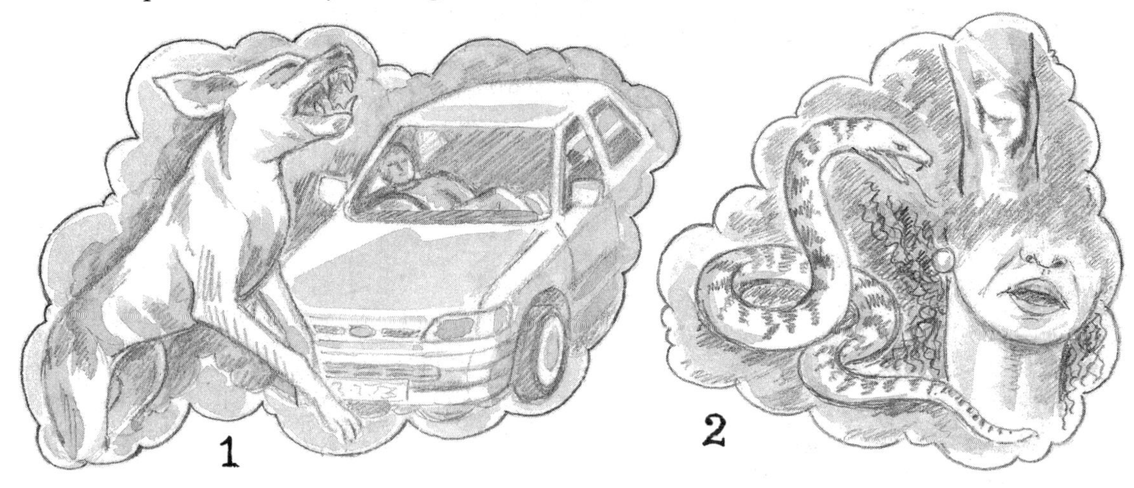

4 Look at these unfinished sentences about the first dream:

1 In his dream, he was in a car that he had when . . .
2 He wasn't sitting in the car, he was . . .
3 He didn't get hurt because . . .

Listen to the man and complete the sentences.

5 Look at these unfinished sentences about the second dream:

1 In her dream, her husband wakes her up when she . . .
2 In her dream she's trying to . . .
3 The snakes are . . .

Listen to the woman and complete the sentences. Compare your sentences with other students. Which of the two dreams do you find more interesting, and why?

B What do dreams mean?

1 Look at these possible explanations of dreams:

a) Dreams predict something in the future.
b) Dreams reveal deep personal anxieties from the past.
c) Dreams translate the physical state of the body into images (for example, if your arm is trapped under your body while you are sleeping, you may dream of being trapped or held).
d) Dreams reveal what is worrying you in the present.
e) Dreams ....

Can you add any other explanation to the list?

2 With another student discuss possible explanations of the man's dream.

Listen to some people talking about this. Which of the explanations in Exercise 1 do they offer? Is your explanation similar?

3 Read this extract from a dictionary of dreams:

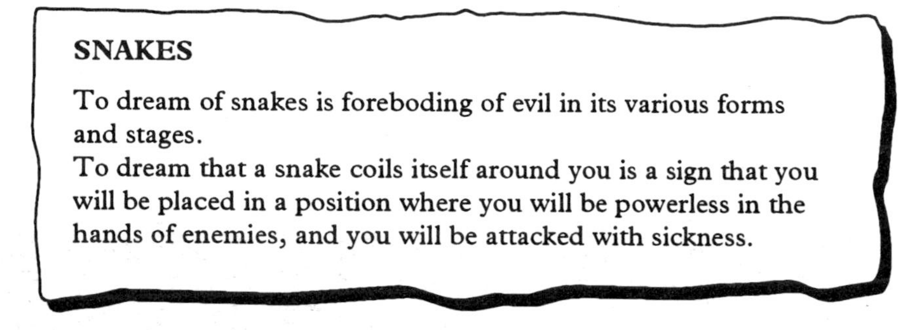

SNAKES

To dream of snakes is foreboding of evil in its various forms and stages.
To dream that a snake coils itself around you is a sign that you will be placed in a position where you will be powerless in the hands of enemies, and you will be attacked with sickness.

Do you think that either of these is a convincing explanation of the woman's dream? Do you have other ideas?

4 Listen to the woman's own explanation of her recurring dream. As you listen, write notes about the three experiences she talks about:

	Where was she?	*What happened?*
Experience 1		
Experience 2	in a convent in the outskirts of the city.	
Experience 3	in a temporary school building.	

Compare notes with another student.

Do you find the woman's explanation a convincing one? Or do you prefer your own?

5 **Extension** Do you have any good explanations for some of your own dreams? In groups, discuss possible explanations.

3 | Puzzles

A I love puzzles and games

1 With a partner, talk about the puzzles and games in the picture. How many can you identify? Do you like puzzles? What kind do you like best? Are puzzles popular in your country?

2 You are going to hear four friends talking about their attitudes to puzzles and games. Which of these do they mention?

	Monopoly	Lateral thinking puzzles		Jigsaw puzzles	Backgam–mon	
Mah–jong						Boggle
Chinese chequers		Trivial Pursuits	Chess	Cross–words		Scrabble

Put a + beside the names of the ones they like; put a – beside the names of the ones they don't like.

3 A student has taken notes on the conversation but has got some things wrong. Can you correct the notes?

Listen to the conversation again if you would like to check your ideas.

Speaker 1: Loves doing crosswords – she's a crossword freak (treat?) Loves all board games, anything like Scrabble and Boggle. Anything to do with birds gives her a lot of pleasure.

Speaker 2: Likes puzzles – loves Trivial Pursuits, ten years after it was invented.

Speaker 3: Can't stand puzzles. Jigsaw puzzles are all the same. Does them with her children. But likes lateral thinking puzzles – on paper. Likes being set a question and having to work it out – doesn't like organised puzzles.

Speaker 4: Asks about Boggle – a game with numbers – you shake them and make words with your hand.

Check your answers with other students.

B Thinking it out

CLUES

Across
3. What you say to your dog when he's too frisky. (3)
5. Some believe that this is what makes people different from animals, but when I hear one after dinner, I wonder. (6)
6. Leave all behind. (7)
7. Criticise, then have a second look. (6)
8. It takes your breath away – so beautiful, or is it painful? (8)

Down
1. Where things go before they come down. (2)
2. Story-telling; a link; a person linked through blood. (8)
3. A cloud's passing over the sun; follow someone secretly. (6)
4. What you are doing now – but can your dog do it as well? (8)
6. Fully awake and attentive, and get others to be the same. (5)

■	1	■	2 R	■	3 S	I	4 T
5 S	P	E	E	C	H	■	
■	■	■	L	■	A	■	
■	6		A		D		
■		■	T	■	O	■	
7			I		W	■	
■		■	O	■	■	■	
8 S	T	U	N	N	I	N	G

1 With a partner, look at the four words that have been written into this puzzle, and find the clues that go with them.

Try to solve number 3 across.

2 Listen to a group of friends trying to solve the puzzle and check your solution.

3 The friends solve three more clues. Listen and write the words in.

4 Now solve number 1 down.

5 There is one clue left. Try to solve it in your group. Then listen to see if you were right. Congratulations! You have completed the puzzle.

4 How do you . . .?

A . . . do the shopping?

Things to buy

1.
2.
3.
4.
5.

1 Write down a list of five things that you need to buy today, or this week. Don't show your list to anyone.

Sit with another student. Try to guess some of the things your partner has listed.

Do you usually make lists before you go shopping at the supermarket? Or are you an 'impulsive' shopper? Discuss this with other students.

2 With a partner, complete the profile of discontented shoppers:

Contented shoppers	*Discontented shoppers*	*The man on the tape*
don't feel the need for a list	....	....
take their time shopping	rush around the shop as quickly as possible	....
are relaxed		—
are in a good mood	....	....
like chatting to people they meet	....	....
	....	....
enjoy looking for bargains	....	—
go home eager to talk about their shopping experiences	go home and forget about it	....
	....	....

3 Listen to a man describing how he shops at a supermarket. Is he a contented or a discontented shopper?

With your partner, fill in as many details as you can for his profile. Listen again if you like and complete the profile.

What about you? What kind of a shopper are you?

4 Listen to a woman talking about shopping at the supermarket. In what ways is she similar to the man?

With a partner, put a tick under the 'yes' column if you agree with the statement below, and a tick under the 'no' column if you disagree. Listen again if necessary.

Statements about the woman on the cassette	*Yes*	*No*
1 She thinks children can be a nuisance in supermarkets.		
2 She's a vegetarian.		
3 She buys frozen food first.		
4 She uses a list.		
5 She likes queuing with a trolley because it's like driving.		
6 The worst thing about shopping for her is getting it all home.		
7 Shopping for her is organised from start to finish.		

Discuss your preferences with others. Which shops are your favourites and why?

B . . . cope with a long journey?

1 What is the longest non-stop journey you've ever been on? Fill in the details:

Place of departure:
Date of departure:
Destination:
Means of transport:
Alone? or with:

Write particular memories from the journey on this line:

Start of journey — End of journey

1 2 3 4 5 6 7 8 9 10 11 12 13 14 15 16 17 18 19 20 21 22 23 24 hours

In small groups, ask each other questions about your longest journey. Did anything exciting happen on any of your journeys? Or were they boring?

2 What do you do to prevent boredom on a long journey? Do you use any of these? Compare your ideas with those of your partner.

3 Listen to someone talking about what he does on a journey. Note the items which he uses.

Does he enjoy travelling?

Here is a flow chart of the speaker's attitude to other people when he is travelling. Complete as many parts as you can:

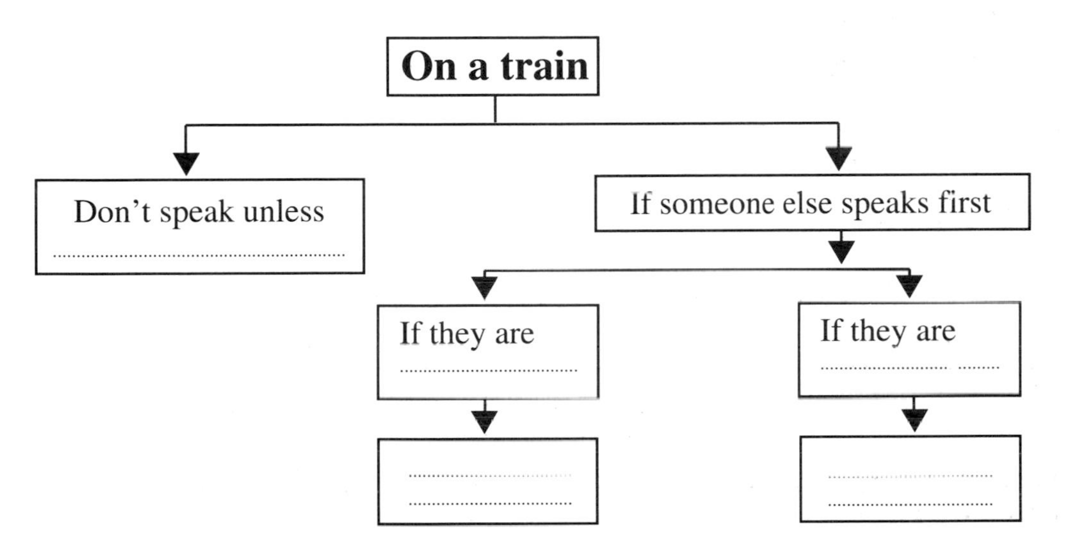

Listen again if you need to. Check and complete your answers.

How do you interpret these things that are said in the conversation? Choose the best interpretation from the box for each statement, or provide your own.

1 'It might be another English thing.'
2 'They might think I'm just taking liberties.'
3 'Don't invade my space.'

a) English people are probably not very friendly to strangers.
b) English people are reserved.
c) English people are sensitive about their privacy.
d) Talking to strangers is rude.
e) English people don't like to get too close physically to other people in public.
f) People don't like losing control of their situation.

4 **Extension** Are you the kind of person who:

a) starts a conversation with strangers?
b) responds if someone else starts up the conversation?
c) keeps yourself to yourself?

How many (a), (b) or (c) people are there in your class?

Are you more likely to engage in conversation with strangers on a train? a plane? a coach? or when hitch-hiking?

5 National anthems

A A rousing tune

1 Can you guess what national anthem this is? Can anyone in the class sing it?

Here are some words that describe national anthems. With a partner, choose at least nine of the words and put each word into one of the three columns. Use a dictionary or ask the teacher if you need help.

solemn a simple tune militaristic lyrical serious funny
old-fashioned rhythmic long boring rousing beautiful
moving silly jingoistic splendid religious memorable
dreadful represents the people important

Positive	*Negative*	*Neutral*
....	....	....
....	....	....
....	....	....

Tell your partner about your own national anthem. If you are all from the same country, talk about your national anthem in groups.

2 Read the six statements below.

Speaker 1: a) Our anthem represents a new African nation.
b) The music makes me go very quiet.
Speaker 2: a) It's not a great song, but I do find it moving.
b) It's not an easy tune to remember.
Speaker 3: a) The new national anthem is very short.
b) The national anthem has many different sorts of tunes and textures.

Now listen to three people talking about their national anthems, and tick three statements which are similar to what they say.

Check your answers with a partner.

3 Listen to the three speakers again and fill in as many details as you can in the grid:

	Words/expressions used to describe the anthem
Speaker 1	
Speaker 2	
Speaker 3	

B Editing a radio programme

Is national pride disappearing?

What do people feel nowadays about their country? Do they still respond with pride to their national anthems? Or are we moving into a new age of internationalism? Do we still celebrate our own country's achievements, for example in sports? Or do we look towards the things that unite the people of the world rather than separate them?

Listen to an international panel discussing these ideas. Chairing the discussion is

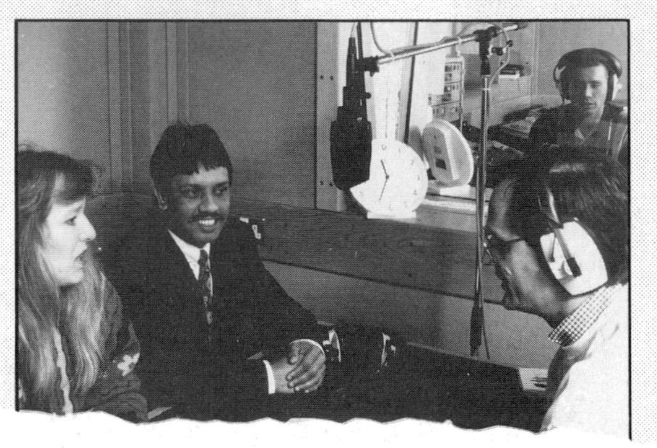

1 Read the description of the radio programme called 'Is national pride disappearing?' Imagine that you are editing the recorded material for it. There are two recorded conversations available, but there is only time to use one on the programme.

Half the class: Listen to conversation 1.

The other half: Listen to conversation 2.

Take notes about the main ideas discussed in the conversation you listen to. Discuss your notes with others in your half of the class. How well does your conversation match the description of the radio programme?

Give it a rating from 0 to 5 for:

Interest (0 = boring, 5 = very interesting)
Usefulness for the radio programme (0 = doesn't match the programme's themes, 5 = very relevant)

2 Join a person who listened to the other conversation. Compare your notes and your ratings.

3 Listen to the other conversation (or listen to both). Decide which of the conversations you prefer. As a class, vote for one of these recommendations:

a) Use conversation 1 for the radio programme.
b) Use conversation 2 for the radio programme.
c) Record some other material.

4 **Extension** To what degree are you a nationalist or an internationalist? Discuss your ideas. (If your class voted for recommendation (c), record your discussion!)

6 Crime and punishment

A A morbid interest?

1 People are often fascinated by crime, and especially by murder. Why do you suppose this is the case?

With a partner, complete the sentence:

People are often fascinated by crime because…

You can consider some of these ideas if you like:

- our ordinary lives are dull, whereas crime is unusual and exciting
- we fear the evil side of our own natures
- trying to solve crimes is like solving puzzles

Compare your sentences with others in the class and talk about them.

2 Listen to someone describing his reaction to a television programme about a serious crime. Add some details to these notes:

On the one hand, he is interested in crime, finds the scientific work of finding clues fascinating, has a curiosity about murders.
On the other hand, he ....
....

Compare your notes. Do you have mixed feelings towards TV programmes about crimes like murder?

3 **Extension** Do you share the man's fascination with crime and crime-solving? Which of these do you enjoy?

- TV documentaries on serious crime
- feature films about murderers
- police or detective novels

Compare your ideas with others in the class. Do you feel that you could ever be capable of committing murder? If so, under what circumstances?

B Make the punishment fit the crime

1 Talk about these questions with other students:

- How are murderers punished in your country?
- What do you think is the best way of dealing with this kind of crime?
- Are some categories of murder more terrible than others? If so, which ones?
- Are there special circumstances (attenuating circumstances) which mean that a murderer should be treated more leniently? If so, which ones can you think of?

2 Look at these expressions from three crime reports. Make sure you understand them. Use a dictionary or ask the teacher if you need to.

a jury   a high court   an unacceptable decision   choke to death
an absolute disgrace   a brain tumour   surgery
smothered with a pillow   put on probation   arson   remorse

3 Look at these newspaper headlines. What can you guess about each crime? The expressions from the crime reports (Exercise 2) might give you some ideas.

Student A	Student B	Student C
Judge frees killer - row rages on	**Mother who killed child referred for psychiatric care**	**Woman put on probation after cat saves man she tried to kill**
Murderer: *Captain Dulaita*	Murderer: *Martha Rudven*	Accused: *Gretta Lanski*
Person killed:	Person killed:	Victim:
Circumstances:	Circumstances:	Circumstances:
Sentence given by judge:	Sentence given by judge:	Sentence given by judge:

4 Work in groups of three. You will hear radio reports about the three crimes. Each group will listen to one of the crimes:
Student A: Take notes on the first crime.
Student B: Take notes on the second crime.
Student C: Take notes on the third crime.

5 Join another group of three students. Compare your notes with the other person who took details on your case. Discuss the sentence passed on the murderer. Do you think it was the right one?

When you are ready, discuss the three cases with the whole group.

7 | Memorable parties

A What I enjoy most about parties is . . .

1 With one or two other students, talk about the sorts of parties that are popular in your country – perhaps you have wedding parties or birthday parties.

Think about the last enjoyable party you went to. Make a short list of the things you enjoyed about it:

I enjoyed ....
I enjoyed ....
I enjoyed ....

Compare your list with others.

2 Listen to two people talking about parties. Write down some of the things they enjoy most.

Compare your notes with others. Did the speakers mention things you listed in Exercise 1?

3 Listen to two more people discussing parties. Tick the views which are mentioned.

a) Parties are good because they release people from the social conventions of everyday life.
b) Smashing windows at parties is a good way of letting go.
c) Alcohol is vital for a good party.
d) Sometimes you enjoy parties you didn't really want to go to.

Do you remember hearing any other views on the cassette? Which views do you agree with?

4 **Extension** Some of the speakers express the view that parties enable people to 'let go' or escape the constraints of everyday life.

To what extent is this important in your own culture?

Do people in your country view parties in this way?

B What a party!

1 At a 'fancy dress party' people dress up in unusual clothes. Sometimes they hire costumes (police uniforms, gorilla or clown costumes, for example) or wear school uniforms or masks.

With other students, talk about parties in your country that are similar to 'fancy dress parties'. Do such parties exist? Are they popular?

2 You are going to hear a woman talking about a fancy dress party that she went to. At this party she got very embarrassed.

Before listening, look at these short extracts from her story:

'. . . I arrived, terribly proud of myself . . .'
'. . . casually dressed in jeans and sweaters . . .'
'. . . she had to lend me something casual to dress in . . .'
'I felt terribly terribly exposed . . .'

Think about the extracts and in groups, try to guess what happened to make her so embarrassed.

Now listen. Were your guesses accurate?

3 How would you feel if you went to a party where most people were deaf? What differences would you expect to find? Compare your thoughts.

Listen to a woman talking about a party for a deaf couple. As you listen, try to answer these questions:

What was the reason for the party?
How were the deaf people able to dance so well?
Why was the woman so impressed with the party?

4 **Extension** Does anyone in your class have a story about an unusual party? Tell the class.

Optional listening. An unusual party story.

8 Babies, brothers and sisters

A Where were you born?

1 Where were you born?

- in hospital?
- at home?
- somewhere else? (in an ambulance? a taxi?)

Do you know anyone who was born in an unusual place, for example while their parents were on holiday or in a distant country?

Talk about your answers with other students.

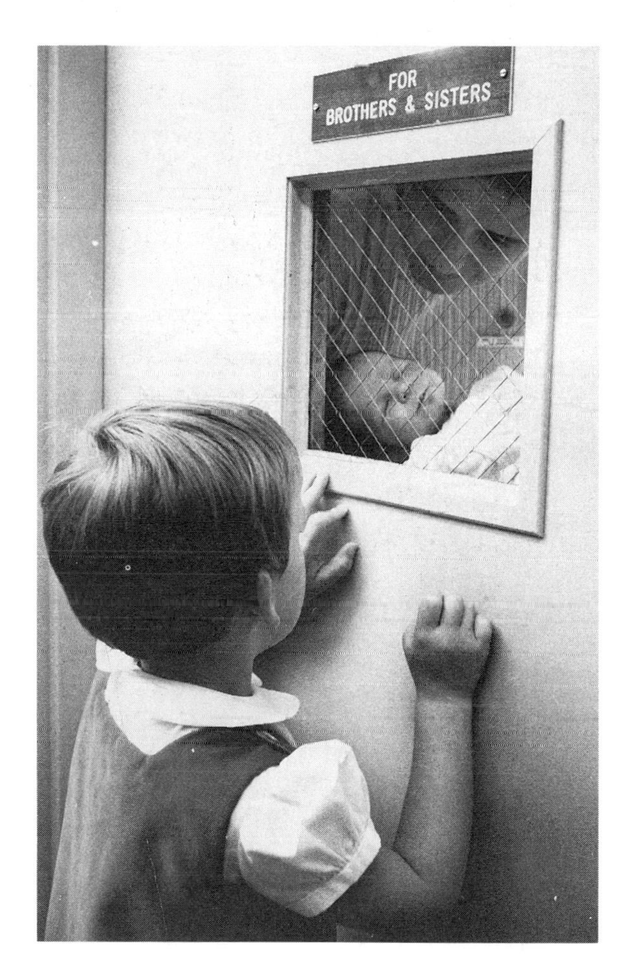

2 Which of these do you think are true?

a) In Australia, most babies are born . . .
at home? *or* in hospital?

b) In Australia, most doctors . . .
encourage women to have babies at home?
or discourage women from having babies at home?

You are going to listen to an extract from an interview with two midwives from Australia. They are talking about births at home and in hospital.

Listen and confirm your guesses. Fill in the details they mention about the different places you can have a baby.

Listen again if you wish to.

Birthing centres	*Having a baby at home*	*Having a baby in hospital*

3 You are going to hear two people giving accounts of their own experiences. After you have listened to both, jot down at least one thing you found interesting or unusual in each account.

Speaker 1 – in hospital

....

Speaker 2 – at home

....

Compare your notes with others in the class.

4 **Optional extension** What is the pattern in your country? Are most babies born at home? Are you aware of any changes in the pattern?

B Brothers and sisters

1 In small groups, talk about this question: If you could redesign the family you grew up in, how many brothers and sisters would you have and what would be the age differences between them?

2 Listen to a woman remembering a childhood incident involving her younger brother. What did she do and why?

Does anyone in your class remember a similar sort of childhood incident?

3 The conversation you have just heard continues. Listen and decide whether these statements are true or false:

1 There are eight years between the two brothers in the family.
2 The speaker is two years younger than her older brother.
3 The youngest child ignored his brother and sister.
4 The two older children were closer to each other.
5 The younger brother left home when he was fifteen.
6 The older brother went to live in Brazil.
7 The speaker went to her younger brother's wedding.
8 The man in the photograph was the speaker's brother.

Compare your answers.

4

Now listen to the rest of the conversation and fill in the speech bubbles for the three children.

5 **Extension** What about your family? Do you have different recollections of the past you shared?

9 Brief encounters

A I couldn't take my eyes off him

Charlie Chaplin
General de Gaulle
Indira Gandhi
Nelson Mandela
Marilyn Monroe
Dame Kiri Te Kanawa

1 Look at these photographs of famous people. With another student try to match the names and the faces and then say what you know about each person.

2 How would you react if you met someone famous? Choose some of the sentences from this list or add your own:

I would be shy.
I would be speechless.
I would be riveted to the spot.
I would just stare.
I would try to be witty.
I would just be natural.
I would . . .
I would . . .

3 You are going to hear two people talking about their encounters with two well-known people from England. As you listen, write notes in the grid. Then compare notes with other students.

Name	*Occupation*	*Where did speaker meet/see him?*	*Speaker's reactions*
Gordon Banks Ray Davies			

4 When people are speaking conversational English spontaneously, they often use little expressions to give themselves more time to say what they want to say. Listen to the two speakers again. How many times does each of them use these expressions:

	Speaker 1	*Speaker 2*
'you know . . .' 'kind of . . .' 'sort of . . .'		

In your own language do you use expressions such as these frequently, or do you use fewer words of this type in conversation? Compare your thoughts with one or two other students. Make a list of some of the 'filler' expressions that you use in your language, then talk to other students for a few moments in your own language and try to use them.

B He had this shock of electricity type hair

1 Have you heard of these two American celebrities? What do you know about them?

Paul Newman

Jimi Hendrix

You will hear the following expressions when you listen. Before listening, try to match the expressions with the photos:

	Paul Newman	*Jimi Hendrix*
a) I met this man who was only five foot seven and a half. b) He must be about sixty now. c) He's in extremely good shape. d) He is rather gorgeous. e) He's not five foot two, he's a good five ten. f) He had this shock of electricity type hair. g) . . . with this just white fluff of hair . . .		

2 Now listen to someone describing the night he met Jimi Hendrix. As you listen, try to answer these questions:

1 How tall was Jimi Hendrix?
2 What did Jimi say in response to these three requests? (Make notes as you listen.)

	Jimi said
'I must have your autograph?'	....
'. . . What is that chord you're playing in *Foxy Lady*?'	....
'How can I learn to play like you?'	....

How would you describe the speaker's attitude towards Jimi Hendrix?

3 Listen to a woman describing the time she met Paul Newman during some rehearsals in a theatre. Divide into two groups and as you listen:

One half of the class makes notes on Paul Newman's physical appearance.
The other half makes notes on the woman's actions, feelings and reactions.

Find someone who was in the other half, and see how much they know about your notes.

Which famous actor or musician would you most like to meet?

What questions would you ask her/him?

4 **Extension** Some people dream of being famous. Describe the things that make fame attractive to you, and those things that would worry you about fame. Make two lists with another student:

Fame is attractive because...
Fame would worry me because...

Compare lists with other pairs. Do you agree?

10 The hole

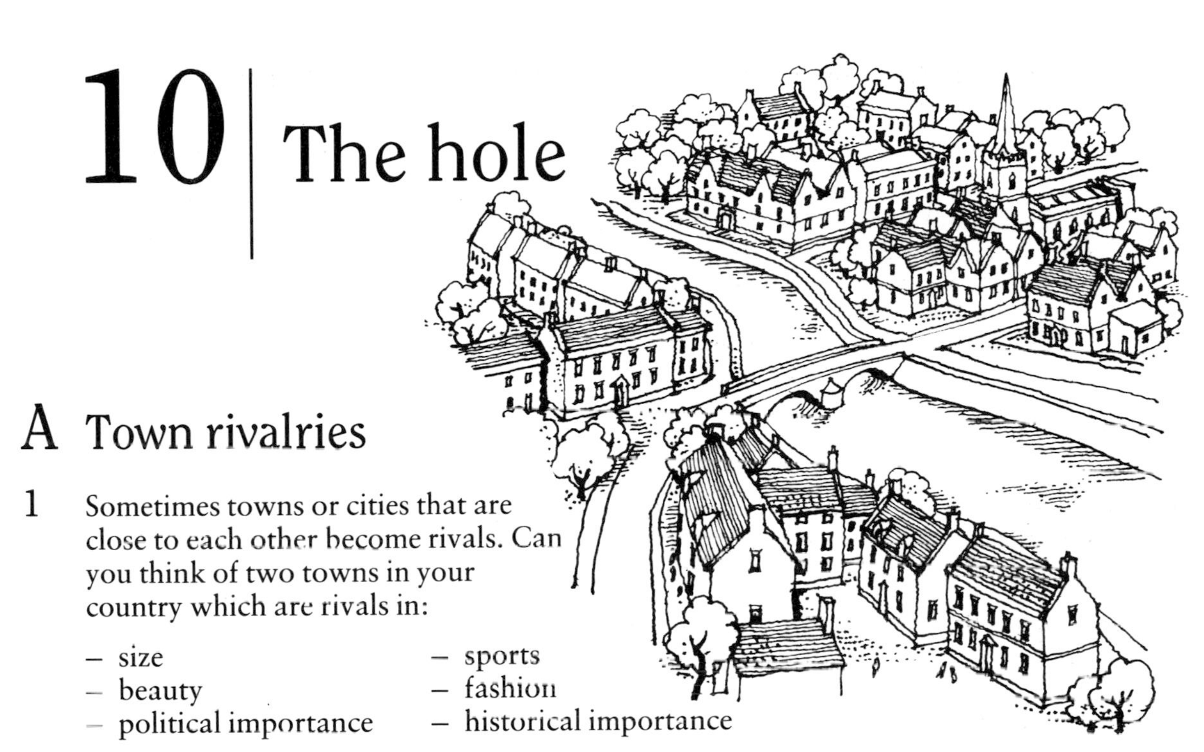

A Town rivalries

1 Sometimes towns or cities that are close to each other become rivals. Can you think of two towns in your country which are rivals in:

- size
- beauty
- political importance
- sports
- fashion
- historical importance

What about your own town, city or village? Does it have a rival? How does this kind of rivalry manifest itself?

2 Imagine this situation: two small towns on opposite sides of a river are joined by a bridge. The bridge has a hole in it. Will the people in the two towns have disagreements?

Compare your ideas with others in the class.

B The hole

1 Listen to Part 1 of the short story, called 'The hole'. It took place last century. Work with a partner.

Partner A:

Jot down notes about the right-bank town.
It thought that it was superior because:
....
....
It thought the hole should be mended by: ....

Partner B:

Jot down notes about the left-bank town.
It thought that it was superior because:
....
....
It thought the hole should be mended by: ....

Check your answers if necessary. How do you think the dispute can be resolved?

If your town asked you for advice, what would you say?

2 Part 2. Look at these unfinished summary sentences. Can you guess how each one could be completed?

Then listen to Part 2 of the story and complete the sentences. Were your guesses right?

1 One day a tramp fell into the hole and ....
2 The people from both towns wanted to know whether he was walking from .... to the left, or vice versa.
3 He could not remember, because ....

The situation is obviously getting worse for both towns. How do you think the story is likely to develop from this point?

3 Part 3. Look at the pictures. They are not in the right order. What do you think happens next in the story? With a partner, can you work out a suitable order?

Listen to the next part. Confirm the right order for the pictures, and complete the sentences:

1 When his coach and horses fell into the hole, the traveller was ....
2 He said he was willing to ....
3 The people of both towns declared that they ....
4 To prove it, they both ....
5 The traveller said he could not see any ....

Compare your sentences with others in the class.

4 Part 4. Here are two key words from the final section: *reconciled* and *harmony*. What do you think the end of the story is going to be?

Listen to the final section.

C Reaction

1 Listen to four people talking about their reactions to the story. What details can you add?

	Reactions
Speaker 1	couldn't understand ending
Speaker 2	quite amusing, admired the wily traveller, it's a little morality tale
Speaker 3	can believe the self-interest of the villagers
Speaker 4	interested to find out ending

What do you think about the reactions of these listeners? Are your reactions similar?

They are puzzled by the ending. Were you?

2 The speakers wonder about the story's moral. Are any of the following possible morals for the story? Add your own if you like.

Human nature is naturally cruel.
People always get their revenge.
An outside threat can reconcile even the worst enemies.
Other: ....

What does your class think?

3 Optional listening. Listen to the whole story again if you like.

11 Teeth and dentists

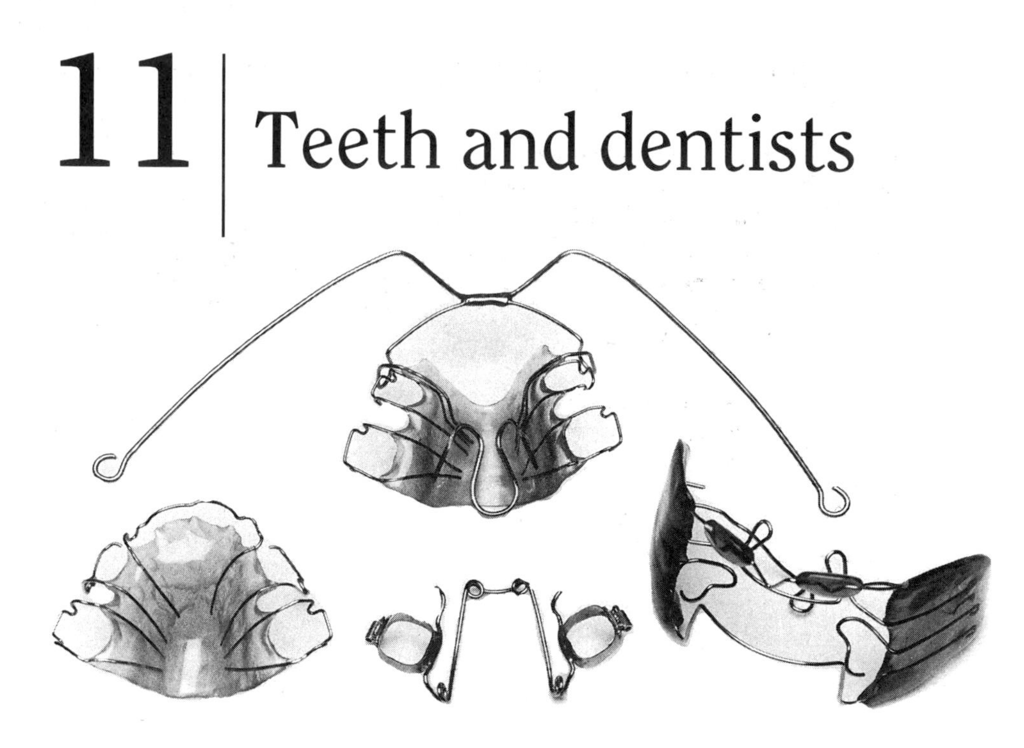

A Childhood memories

1 What do you think these items might be used for?

2 Listen to three people talking about their teeth, and what happened to them as children. How many details can you add to this grid?

	Problem	*What was done*
Speaker 1		lots of wire bands round her teeth
Speaker 2	bad teeth	
Speaker 3	two prominent front teeth	

3 Listen to the three people as they continue talking about their experiences. Some of their memories are positive (+) and some are negative (−). Note down two positive memories and two negative memories:

+	−
....	....
....	....

4 **Extension** Do you have memories from your childhood concerning teeth? They could be positive or negative memories. Share them with others.

B Vivid experiences at the dentist's

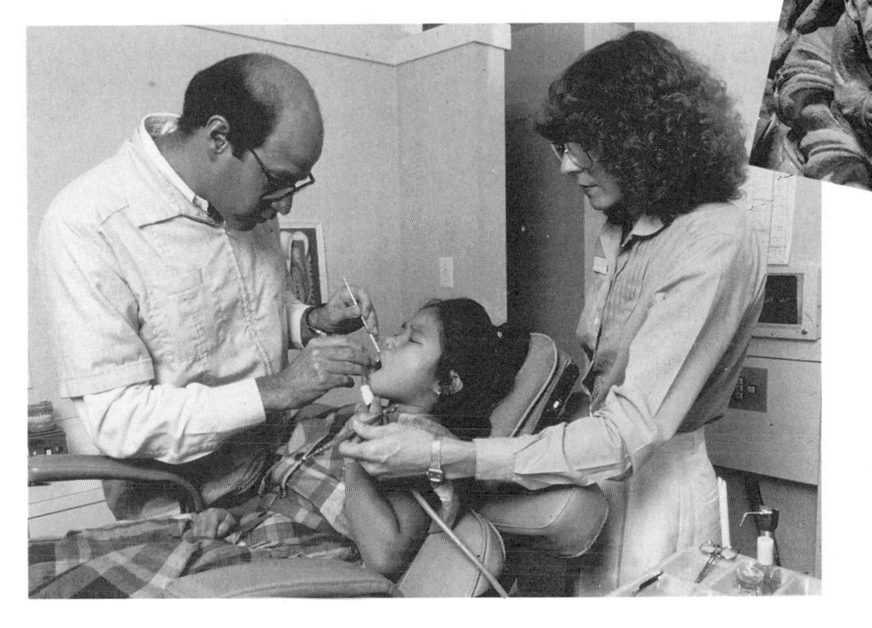

'Man with a Toothache'
(Wells Cathedral)

1 What is your present attitude to going to the dentist? Fill in the questionnaire:

1 When was the last time you went to a dentist?

- ☐ within the last six months
- ☐ between six months and one year ago
- ☐ between one and two years ago
- ☐ between two and five years ago
- ☐ between five and ten years ago
- ☐ over ten years ago or never

2 What is your attitude to these statements? Tick one of the two boxes:

	definitely	*to some extent*
i) I'm nervous of some dental treatments.	☐	☐
ii) The worst part of going to the dentist is waiting.	☐	☐
iii) I always feel very anxious about going to the dentist.	☐	☐
iv) If I had toothache, I'd take pain-killers rather than go to the dentist.	☐	☐
v) Going to the dentist is a cold, clinical, impersonal experience.	☐	☐

3 Are you satisfied with your teeth? Yes ☐ No ☐

Compare your answers with others, and discuss possible reasons for your attitudes. (If you would like to know how a survey of British people answered this questionnaire, look at the Key.)

2 Which of these expressions describe how you react at the dentist's?

I feel faint   my hands go white at the knuckles   I become hysterical

my toes turn up   my arms go rigid   I get a headache   I throw up

I pass out   I scream   I'm extremely brave   I'm quite relaxed

I think of something else   I have gas or an injection to avoid pain

I have no feelings at all   I enjoy talking to the dentist

Others: ....

Compare your reactions with others in the class and talk about any vivid experiences you remember.

3 Listen to a person talking about her most vivid dental experience. Which of the above reactions does the speaker mention happening to her?

4 Is dentistry a profession that attracts you? Why? Or why not?

Listen to one man giving a very personal view of the job. Can you offer any counter arguments to give a more positive view of dental work?

5 **Extension** Listen to an anecdote about a Canadian dentist. Imagine that it is to be published in a magazine. With a partner, make up an attractive title for the anecdote.

12 Take our advice

A Learning to drive

Examination questions

To complete your test you will be asked to write in the box next to the question numbers listed on the Answer Card an appropriate letter (A, B, C, or D) as shown against the answer you think is correct.

Which vehicles are required to give way in these two examples?

A – Vehicle B in case 1 and Vehicle A in case 2
B – Vehicle B in both cases
C – Vehicle A in both cases

Case 1
Divided Road
A
Dividing Crossover Strip
B

Case 2
A
B

What does this sign mean if used with a stop line painted on the road?

A – Stop if any traffic is approaching from the right
B – Stop if there is any traffic on the intersection
C – Stop at the stop line and give way to vehicles approaching from any other direction
D – Slow down and drive carefully

1 The questions above are from the Australian driving test where drivers drive on the left side of the road. What do you know about the driving test in your country and other countries? Talk about:

- what you have to do during the road test.
- the questions on the written test, if there is one.
- the cost of the test.
- the number of lessons you generally need before you take the test.
- books and cassettes you can buy to help you pass.

2 You are going to hear a cassette called 'How to pass the driving test'. It is used in Britain by people who are learning to drive.

- If you are a driver, imagine that you have bought it for a friend.
- If you are a non-driver, imagine that it is going to help you to learn to drive.

Before you listen, look at these statements. Which ones do you think you will probably hear in the first minute of the cassette?

a) Use this tape to practise driving.
b) Use this tape while you are driving your car.
c) This tape will help you to pass your driving test.
d) This tape is all you need to pass your driving test.
e) You only need to listen once, then you'll have a good chance of passing first time.
f) Use the tape every time you practise.
g) Learning to drive is easy! Even a child could do it.

Listen to the tape. Were you right?

What do you think of the way the tape is introduced? Was it: interesting? lively? useful? patronising?

3 Listen to some instructions on how to hold the steering wheel. As you listen, label the wheels in the diagram, from 1 to 3. Then compare your answers with others.

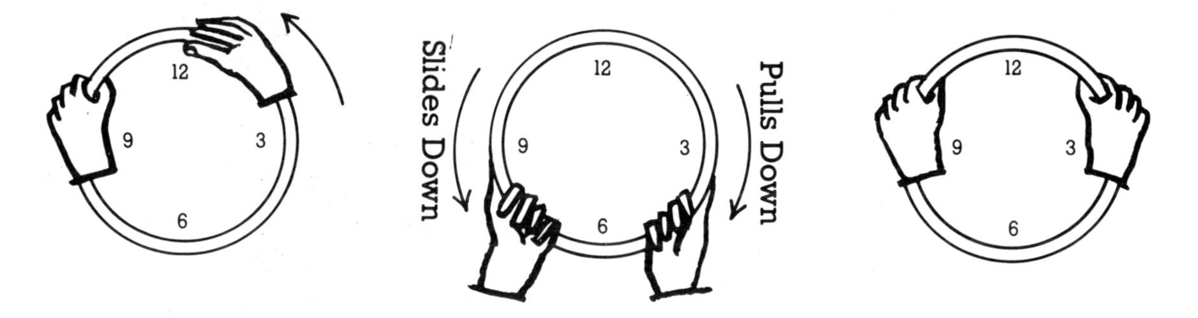

4 **Extension** Talk about these questions in small groups:

1 Are you good at following instructions? Have you ever had problems with instruction booklets when you:
   – bought a new appliance, e.g. a watch with many functions or a video recorder?
   – tried to build something from a kit?
   – tried to do something the first time, e.g. doing keep fit exercises, changing a flat tyre?
2 Do you prefer instructions with or without diagrams?
3 Would you prefer just a booklet, or a booklet with a cassette?
4 When you visit museums or art exhibitions, do you like using a recorded tour on cassette?

B Starting a business

1 Imagine that you and your partner have decided to start a small business. You are keen but haven't had any previous experience. Consider these two questions. Use some of the ideas listed if you like.

How do you feel about starting your business?	*What do you do first?*
worried naive about business happy to be my own boss	see the bank manager take out a loan make a business plan ask friends for advice

2 You are going to hear part of a cassette developed by one of the major banks in Britain, to help people who are starting up in business.

Listen to the two presenters interviewing four people. Fill in the missing details:

	What they felt like when they started	*What they did first*
Speaker 1		
Speaker 2		
Speaker 3		
Speaker 4		

Compare your views from Exercise 1 with those you've heard on the tape.

3 One of the major problems experienced by people in business is 'bad debt', that is, they cannot get their customers to pay up! Alan was the first person interviewed on this cassette. He set up a business making and selling 'Yorkshire fancies' (special little cakes). You will hear him talking about his problems with bad debts. Before you listen, try to sort out the following sentences into two groups:

– Sentences that describe how the problem happened.
– Sentences that describe what Alan did about it.

a) He noticed that two customers had not paid.
b) He asked his main suppliers to give him longer term for credit.
c) He went to the bank manager and got a longer term on his overdraft.
d) He phoned the troublemakers.
e) He did very well, business was booming.
f) He finally got the customer to pay.
g) He got his solicitor to write to the troublemaker.
h) He got so busy he neglected his invoicing.

Listen and check to see if you were right.

4 Finally, listen to the advice the bank gives about this situation. Which piece of advice do you consider to be the most valuable? What did you think of the way the advice was presented on this cassette?

In this unit, you've heard extracts from two quite different instruction cassettes. Which did you prefer? Why?

Compare your thoughts with others in the class.

5 **Extension** Would you consider starting up your own business? If so, what would you make or sell?

13 Emotions

A Crying

1 What do you feel about crying? Fill in this questionnaire:

		Yes	*No*
1	Do you feel guilty if you cry in public?	☐	☐
2	Do you think that crying is a sign of weakness?	☐	☐
3	Do you think that men and boys should be encouraged to hide their tears?	☐	☐
4	Do you feel embarrassed if you find yourself crying while watching a film?	☐	☐
5	Would you try to hold back your tears at a funeral?	☐	☐
6	Would you distrust a politician who cried in public?	☐	☐
7	Do you think tears are an unnecessary expression of emotion?	☐	☐
8	Would you allow someone to comfort you if you were found crying?	☐	☐
9	Do you get embarrassed if you see an adult crying?	☐	☐
10	Would you pretend you had something in your eye if someone saw you crying?	☐	☐

2 Now turn to the Key to find your score and what the score means. With others in the class, discuss the questionnaire. Do you think that your profile is accurate? Do you think that the advice given in the profiles is right and useful?

3 Listen to three speakers making statements about when they cry. Draw a line between each speaker and the expressions they use, and complete the parts that are missing:

	more so during bereavement
Speaker 1	at sad ....
Speaker 2	at my own life
Speaker 3	I .... easily
	at a really sad ....
	at the life of .... s
	at the birth of a baby

4 Listen to the speakers as they continue to talk. How many of these questions can you answer about each one?

Speaker 1
How does she feel when she lets her emotions out?
What does she think about how men and women show their emotions in Great Britain?

Speaker 2
What does he think is typical of his black culture?
What happened when his father died?
Why does he think it is important to grieve publicly?

Speaker 3
When did her feelings about showing emotions change?
What did she have to do to become a counsellor?
What did she discover about herself?

B Anger and how to deal with it

1 Where do people show their anger in public? Write down at least two places where you have seen people getting angry. Compare with other people in the class. Have most people written down the same place?

2 Listen to Breda talking about the place she sees people being angry, in London, the city where she lives. Which of these are views that she expresses?

a) There is a lot of repressed anger in London.
b) People get angry in their cars, which are like closed little containers.
c) People are angry when they see bikes being used in London.
d) Drivers at traffic lights sound their horns louder than anyone else.
e) People get angry when traffic lights turn red.
f) People are furious when other cars do not move quickly when the light turns green.

Do you have similar reactions when you're caught in traffic?

3 Read these two short paragraphs written by wives about the way in which their husbands deal with anger:

Linda: My husband Bill and I react in totally different ways. When something happens that irritates me, I just blow up. One thing that really irritates me is waiting in long queues at the post office, I get really angry, and I tend to make loud insulting remarks. Everybody knows I'm cross. But Bill just waits patiently – he looks the model of patience, you know, and then when he gets up to the counter he says something that's really quite insulting, but he says it sweetly, with a nice smile, as though it were a compliment. And it usually takes people a few minutes to figure out what he means. He thinks that getting angry is silly, childish and that his way is better. But I think he doesn't really get rid of his anger that way – he just stores it up inside.

Marie: *Well, we've both got terrible tempers but I try not to be angry at the same time as him! He's sometimes in a vile mood when he wakes up – it takes a while to coax him out of it. And when he's in a bad mood there's no use trying to reason with him – the best thing is to give him a lot of attention, just be very soothing and patient and make him a nice cup of coffee – and if that doesn't work, just stay out of his way until he feels more human!*

Listen to the husbands talking about how they cope with anger. Are their views of themselves the same as their wives'? Jot down the main differences between the two. Compare your notes with those of other students.

4 How can we cope with anger? Here are some possible strategies. Which works best for you? Add another strategy if you like.

count to ten before you act be sarcastic shout abuse

have a fist fight take it out on people around you kick the cat

write a letter of protest swear a little, you'll feel better

imagine that the person you are angry with is a pillow and punch it

laugh about the whole thing

....

5 Listen to the end of the conversation. Which strategy is seen as the best? Why? What are the benefits it gives?

14 Flirting with danger

A We've had some near misses

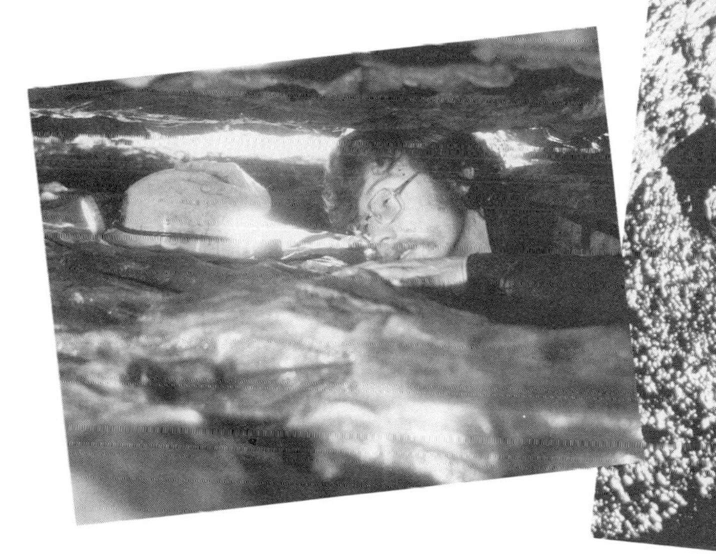

1 Would you be willing to do the kind of thing shown in the pictures? Have you ever been caving? Talk about your experiences – or your reactions to the pictures – with others in the class.

With a partner, look at these pictures. If you are not cavers, try to guess which of these are needed for caving.

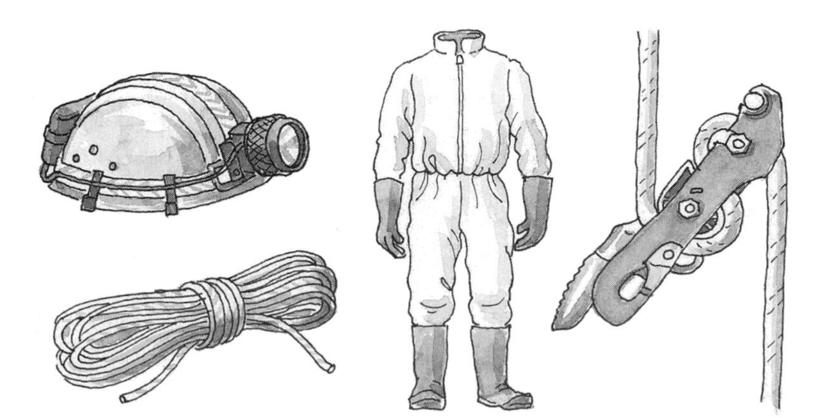

2 Listen to a group of cavers at a dinner party, talking about the equipment you need when you start caving. Look at the pictures in Exercise 1 and tick the equipment mentioned as you listen. Name two other things that are needed but not shown in the picture.

3 Listen to the cavers discussing whether caving is dangerous or not. They cannot agree. What arguments do they use to support their views? Complete the following notes:

It's safe	*What do you mean, it's safe!!*
Caving isn't dangerous compared with...	You're hung by not very much over...
It's unlikely that...	The consequences of having anything other than...

4 As the conversation continues, the cavers remember two accidents they saw in caves. Here are the caving logs (daily written records) for that day.

Listen to the conversation, and complete the entries:

July 22: Accident in Cave 12/5 Pozu de la Cistra. Fred hit directly in the face by a falling stone near cave entrance. Action taken: injured caver helped to surface. Attended by Dr. Rose and Grayson.
Spent night at ....
Next morning: injured caver helped down ....
Put in .... and taken to .... in Oviedo.

August 26: Gavin almost had a serious accident today. Advance party reached the bottom of cave F2 Pozu Los Caracoles. Heard stone rumbling so he moved .... and stone fell ....
A narrow miss!

B It's not inherently dangerous but . . .

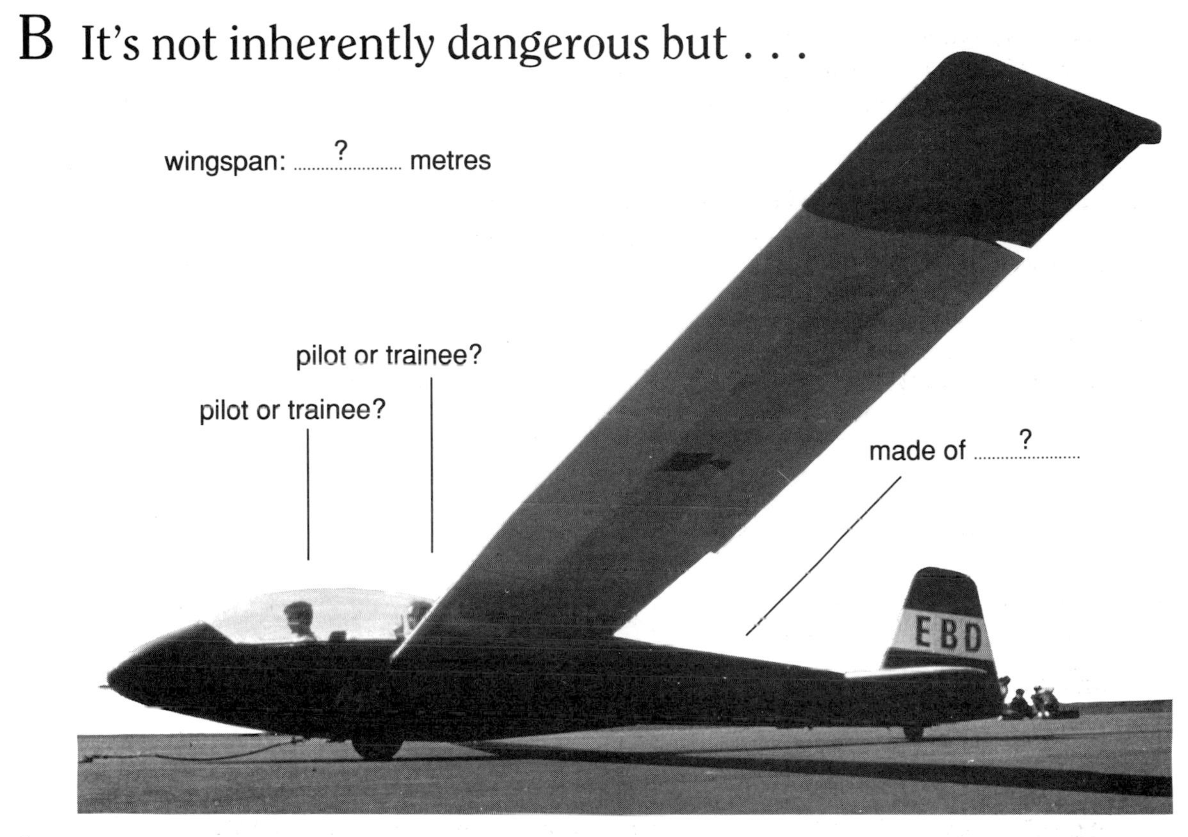

1 What is a glider? How is it different from an aeroplane?

With a partner, try to guess the answers to these other questions about gliders and gliding:

How many hours does it take on average to train to fly a glider on your own?
What is the wingspan of the average glider?
What are gliders made of?
Does the trainee sit behind the instructor or in front of him in the glider?

Listen to an interview with Frank, an Australian gliding instructor. As you listen, complete the gaps in the pictures and see if your guesses were right.

2 Listen to Frank talking about other aspects of gliding. As you listen, make notes under the appropriate headings. Check the meaning of each heading first.

Comfort	*Talking to the pilot*	*Sensations*	*Age*	*Why glide?*

3 Ask other students three of these questions to see if they can supply the answers from their notes:

1 Which jet airliner has less 'elbow room' than a glider?
2 Why does Frank tell his passengers when he is going to be quiet for a while?
3 What does it feel like to be up in a glider?
4 How old is the oldest instructor Frank knows?
5 How old is the oldest pilot Frank knows about and what sort of aircraft does this man fly?
6 What does Frank like about gliding?

Listen again if you need to confirm your answers.

4 **Extension** Would you be willing to sit in the front seat and go on a training flight? Do you think that would be flirting with danger?

15 Feet and walking

A My poor feet

1 Complete the two sentences about your own feet. Use these expressions or your own words if you prefer:

My feet are rather...

Compare your choices with others. Would you like to swap your feet for those belonging to someone else in the class?

2 You're going to listen to three people talking about problems they have with their feet. For each speaker, write down any important words that you catch:

	Problems and features
Speaker 1	Has Piscean feet (Pisces: fish zodiac sign).
Speaker 2	
Speaker 3	He comes from Texas.

Compare your notes with the student next to you. Do any of these people seem to have feet similar to your own?

3

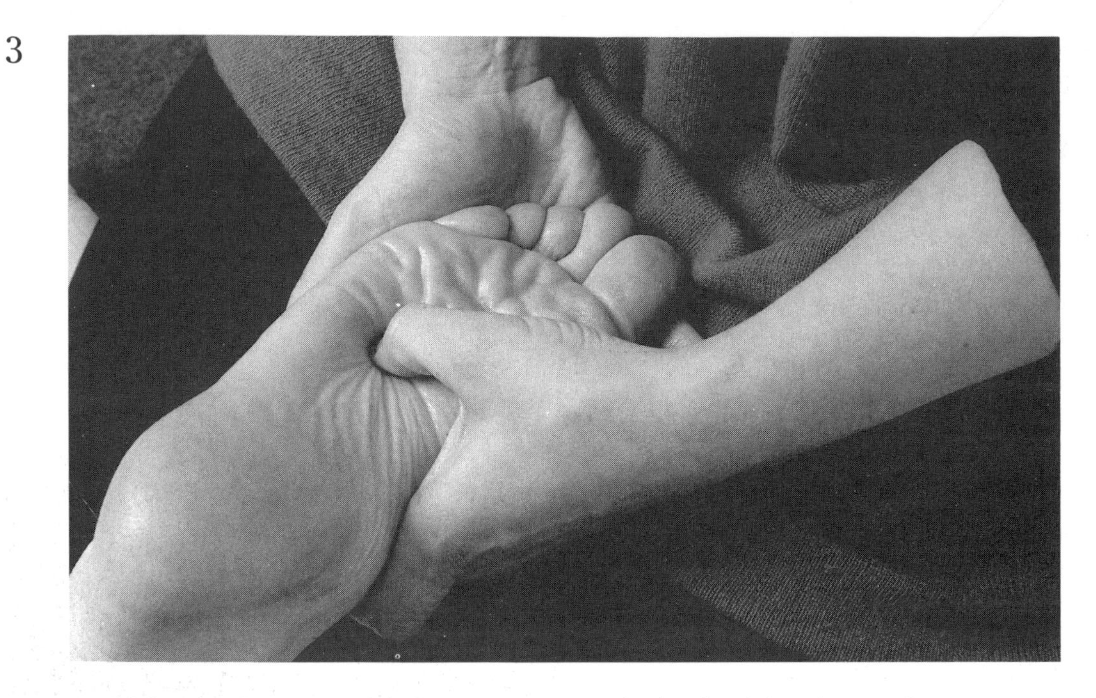

Half the class: go out of the room (or go to the back of the class and cover your ears with your hands), so that you don't hear the recording. When the other half has finished listening, ask at least two of them this question:

What was the man on the cassette saying about feet?

Other half of the class: listen to the man on the cassette. Tell the students who didn't hear it what the man said.

4 Listen again together to see if anything important was missed when you told or were told what the man said.

Do you agree with the man's views?

B Two walking stories

1 Study these words and expressions from a story about sore feet in France. With another student, can you piece together a story from the list?

France	complaining
wealthy family	'We've got something'
courses	room
no vélo (small motorbike)	large box
hilly	creams, salts, elastoplast
blisters	

Listen to the story. In what ways was it similar to your version?

2 Look at these answers to questions about a walk to the top of a mountain in Madeira:

1 It took about eight hours.
2 It was six inches wide.
3 Thousands and thousands of feet.
4 Falling down precipices.
5 In a mountain hut.
6 Very foggy.
7 We felt our way down.

Listen to the story. With a partner, imagine you are talking to the speaker. What seven questions could you ask her/him about the walk in order to get each of those answers? Here is an example:

1 How long did the walk take? It took about eight hours.

Compare your questions with other students. You can listen to the story of the walk again, to check whether your questions are appropriate.

Can you remember any interesting or exciting walks that you've been on? Tell the class about them.

3 **Extension** Think of one place in the world to go for a peaceful walking holiday. Tell another student the name of your chosen place and explain why you have chosen it. Does the idea of a walking holiday appeal to you?

16 Credit cards

A I use mine for . . .

1 Look at the list below. How would you pay for these items? Mark each one with either: C (for cash) *or* Ch (for cheque) *or* CC (for credit card).

food and drink	☐	clothing	☐
travel	☐	theatre tickets	☐
petrol	☐	car repairs	☐
hotels	☐	holiday accommodation	☐
insurance	☐	books	☐
restaurants	☐	fees for courses	☐
records	☐	paper	☐
newspapers	☐	medicines	☐
Others:	☐	....	☐

Find another student who has marked items differently from yours. Compare your ideas about credit cards.

What do you feel about credit cards? Do you think they are:
a useful facility? a temptation to overspend? dangerous?
not necessary?
....

2 Listen to three speakers describing when they use their credit cards. Write down what each one uses their cards for:

Speaker 1: ....

Speaker 2: ....

Speaker 3: ....

Are these uses like your own or different?

3 Here is some advice for credit card users from a booklet published by a consumer association. Read it with another student. What do you think of the advice? Is there anything you think is missing from this list?

1. Keep a close check on what you are spending.
2. Be careful not to get too close to your limit.
3. If you get into trouble, cut your card up.
4. Always make sure you pay your cards off every month. Don't stagger them (that is, don't pay some off one month, keeping the rest to pay later).
5. Be careful not to spend more money than you really have.

4 Listen to two speakers talking about the way they use their credit cards. Which of the five statements in Exercise 3 do the speakers put into practice?

B Anecdotes about credit cards

1 Has anyone in your class ever lost their credit cards or had them stolen? Did any of these things happen?

- The thief used the card quickly before the theft could be reported.
- The owners of the card had to pay for purchases made by the thief.
- The thief got cash from a bank with the card.
- Other: ....

Tell others in the class about the experience.

2 You are going to hear someone talking about the experience of having her cards stolen. Before you listen, study these statements with another student. They are not in the right order. Choose an order for them.

a) Three different people spent over £2,000 using her cards.
b) Someone snatched her handbag in the store.
c) Several people took her cards two miles away.
d) She phoned all the credit card companies.
e) She took out insurance on her cards.
f) Several people went into banks, pretended to be the speaker, and got large sums of cash.
g) She alerted the store security.

Listen to the story and jot down the order in which things happened.

What was the thing which most alarmed her?

3 Listen to another anecdote, this time about someone who does not use credit cards. The speaker is describing an experience he and his friend had in America. Tick the right answer from the ones given. Before you listen, read through the sentences and make sure you understand the alternatives.

1 The speaker and his friend:
   a) were booked into a hotel by friends of theirs.
   b) were booked into a hotel by an American organisation.
   c) booked themselves in and paid for themselves.

2 The hotel:
   a) refused to accept his credit card.
   b) refused to let him sit in the lobby.
   c) refused to let him go to his room.

3 In America, according to the second speaker:
   a) you can't rent a car without a credit card.
   b) you need a number to pay your bills.
   c) you need more than one credit card.

Compare your answers with others.

4 **Extension** In the conversation you've just heard, one speaker says: 'What's underneath that is the society in which you're only good if you have numbers attached to you'.

What is he implying about society? Choose one of these interpretations or write your own:

a) Our society is becoming too materialistic.
b) Our society doesn't value people who are non-conformists.
c) In our society, a person's real character and behaviour are unimportant – all that matters is their ability to pay.
d) Our society has become depersonalised.
e) People are unwilling to help other people.
f) (Write your own:) ....

Compare your answers with others. Do you hold similar views?

17 Friends and friendship

You can't choose your relatives but you can choose your friends. *[Oscar Wilde]*

It's the friends you can call up at 4 a.m. that matter. *[Marlene Dietrich]*

I do not believe that friends are necessarily the people you like best, they are merely the people who got there first. *[Peter Ustinov]*

It is prudent to put the oil of delicate politeness on the machinery of friendship. *[Colette]*

We need two kinds of acquaintance: one to complain to, while we boast to the other. *[Logan Pearsall Smith]*

Having only friends would be dull anyway like eating eggs without salt. *[Hedda Hopper]*

A I value it above everything else

1 Look at these lines showing words used in English for different levels of friendship. How many of them do you know?

stranger acquaintance friend good friend best friend
virtual stranger close acquaintance old friend close friend closest friend

chum (British English) pal close mate best buddy
mate (British & Australian English) buddy (American English) old chum

How many words do you know in your own language that indicate different degrees of friendship? Talk about these words with another student. Are they formal or informal words?

2 Listen to a Scottish man talking about his closest friends.

His best friend is .... because ....

3 Listen to two other people talking about aspects of friendship. As you listen, make notes about anything they say that interests you.

Speaker 1: ....

Speaker 2: ....

Share your notes with another student and discuss your reactions. Are the speakers' views on friends and friendship similar to yours?

4 **Extension**

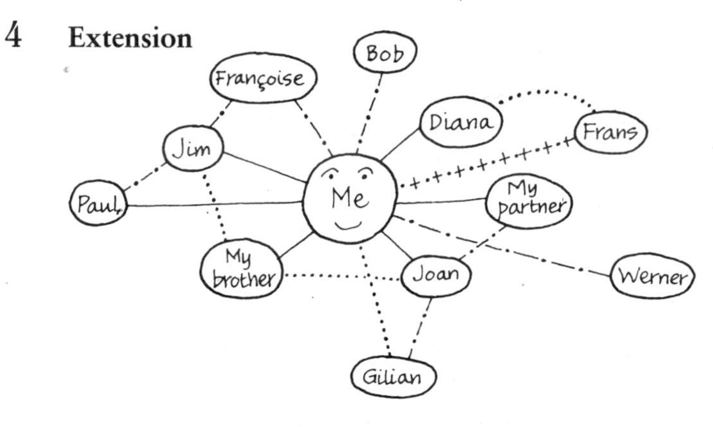

Draw a diagram to show your main friends and how close you feel to each of them. Ask other students questions about the people in their diagrams.

B Losing and keeping friends

1 Why do childhood friends sometimes drift apart? With others, suggest at least two reasons.

Listen to Maggie talking about how she and her very best schoolfriend broke up when they were in their twenties.
What was the main reason for the break-up?
Was this one of the reasons you mentioned?

These mottos about friends and friendship are based on some of the things people said in a conversation.

Listen to it, and with a partner create two more mottos. In groups, compare your mottos.

Make a poster to put up in your class. Write your own motto for it (or use one from the conversation you heard, if you prefer).

3 **Extension** Listen for enjoyment to this song called 'You've got a friend'.

18 Learning languages

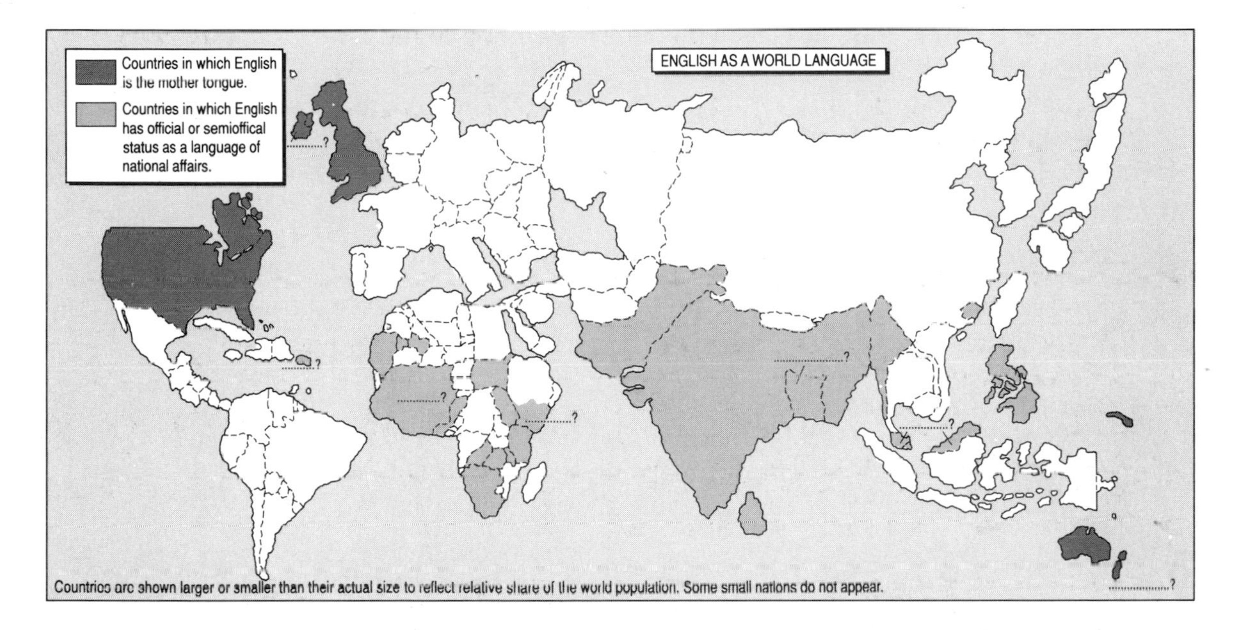

A English, what English?

1 These are some of the countries of the world where English is an official language. Can you supply the missing names?

2 Listen to someone talking about the main language he had to learn. Match the beginnings of his sentences in column 1 with the right endings in column 2:

Column 1	*Column 2*
1 The main language I	a) nobody understands a word I say.
2 I was born in a	b) 'mines' for 'mine' and 'but' at the end of a sentence.
3 When I speak Glaswegian	c) learned was English.
4 When I went to drama school	d) poor area of Glasgow.
5 Glaswegian has dialect words like	e) they laughed at me.

Check your results with another student.

3 The conversation continues. Listen and match the two columns again, but this time some single words have been left out. Fill in the missing information:

1 An Irishman will never use one word	a) the other kids laughed.
2 Irish people say: Hang on a second	b) I had a strong .... accent.
3 Irish people say: It's great to see you and	c) have you got a ....?
4 The Irish and the Scots	d) when he can use ....
5 When I came to England	e) when are you going home?
6 I didn't think much about it but	f) are very ....
7 I noticed that kids in the class with high marks	g) people stopped .... at me.
8 People said to me:	h) I'll be back in a minute.
9 Well I never got high marks but	i) spoke the Queen's ....

Check your results with another student.

4 **Extension** Talk about these questions with others in your class.

Do you have people who speak different languages or different forms of your national language in your country?
Do people in your country sometimes have to learn an 'official' version of their own language?
If so, is there a lot of feeling about this in your country?
What do you think: does having many different kinds of language in a country make it a better and more interesting place to live in?

B I just sort of had to pick it up

1 How many languages have you learnt? ☐ List them: ....
How many can you speak? ☐ List them: ....
How many can you read? ☐ List them: ....

How many languages in all has your class learnt? ☐

2 Listen to two people talking about 'picking up languages'. What languages do they mention? Add other details if you can about how they learnt the languages, and why.

	Language learnt	*How?*	*Why?*
Speaker 1	Spanish	doesn't say	to go on holiday
Speaker 2			

3 Two people talk about their good and bad experiences with language classes at school. Take notes as you listen, then compare with a partner:

- What enjoyable experiences do the speakers remember?
- What did they dislike?
- What languages (if any) did they learn?

4 **Extension** How have you learnt the languages you know?
in classes by living in the country a mixture of both

What works best for you? Compare your experiences with others in the class.

19 | A multicultural world

A Mixed marriages

1 In groups, consider this situation:

A man from your country goes to work in another country with a different language and culture. He gets to know someone at work there and they get married. They return to your country so that she can meet his family.

What might the family and the daughter-in-law be worried about?

What sort of questions might she be asked?

2 You are going to hear a British woman talking about her relationship with her Russian mother-in-law. Look at these sentences and as you listen make notes to complete them:

1 The mother-in-law wanted to know ....
2 The mother-in-law's greatest concern was ....
3 The mother-in-law couldn't understand ....
4 The mother-in-law thought that the woman ....

Compare your sentences with others.

One of the things the woman says about her Russian relatives is: *They met and gave me the going over and within a few hours I was in, I knew I was in.*

In this case the woman was accepted after some questioning. Is this how you imagined the situation developing in your country?

3 You are going to hear another account of meeting in-laws. What were the main issues here and how did things change?

4 The people in this conversation talk next about the benefits which mixed marriages offer. Which benefits do they mention?

B Distant relatives

1 Ask two other students in your class these questions:

Do you have relatives who live far away?
Do you see them often?
Do you keep in touch? How?

Get into small groups and compare your answers.

2 You will hear someone speaking about her family, which is spread all over the world. List the countries where she has relatives.

How does her family keep in contact? Tick the ways she mentions:

☐ speaking on the telephone ☐ visiting cousins ☐ weddings
☐ writing letters ☐ meeting once a year ☐ meeting once a week
☐ celebrations for birthdays Others: ....

Check your answers with another student.

3 Listen to someone who was born in Texas, in the United States, but now lives in England. Make notes as you listen about:

- how he feels about being away from his family.
- the difficulties his grandmother has when she visits him.

4 **Extension** Do any of you have stories to tell about the first time you visited another country? What things did you find most confusing?

20 Ngarrindjeri

A Aboriginal people in Australia

1 How much do you know about Aborigines in Australia? With a partner talk about them, then choose answers to these questions:

1 Of the population of Australia today, people of Aboriginal descent comprise about
  a) five per cent
  b) two per cent
  c) ten per cent
2 It is believed that the Aborigines
  a) have always been in Australia.
  b) came to Australia about 100,000 years ago.
  c) came at least 30,000 years ago.
3 How many distinct Aboriginal languages are there?
  a) five
  b) 50
  c) 300

4 What is a 'didjeridu'?
   a) A dance performed by Aboriginal men.
   b) A type of musical instrument.
   c) A ceremonial spear.

5 When white settlers came to Australia, the numbers of Aborigines
   a) increased significantly.
   b) stayed about the same.
   c) decreased dramatically.

6 Aborigines received the right to vote in Australia in the
   a) 1930s.
   b) 1950s.
   c) 1960s.

Talk about your answers with another pair and then check the Key.

2 You are going to listen to an Aboriginal woman, Doreen Kartinyeri. Doreen belongs to the Ngarrindjeri people of South Australia. After her mother died, she lived in a Salvation Army hostel and now works in the Museum of South Australia. The tape that you will hear is the one that is used by visitors to that museum.

Doreen is interviewed about her own family.

Listen and fill in the missing information:

1 She has .... children.
2 She has been foster mother to .... children.
3 She has .... grandchildren.

3 Doreen goes on to explain why she fostered so many Aboriginal children. What do you think some possible reasons might be? Talk about this question with another student.

Listen to the interview. What three reasons does Doreen give?

1 ....
2 ....
3 ....

Could you foster children? Under what circumstances would you be prepared to look after someone else's children? Discuss this question with other students.

4 Doreen tells a story about the Christian settlers trying to change tribal ways in the nineteenth century. Read these sentences carefully. One of them is false. Which one do you think it is?

With another student, change the sentence you think is false, so that the story makes sense.

1 The Reverend Taplin stopped the Aborigines on the mission from having more than one wife.
2 William had to choose between his two wives.
3 He decided to choose Jane because she was the younger wife.
4 Jane went back to her family.
5 Jane's family felt dishonoured by William's decision.
6 Jane's family felt they had to kill William's father.
7 The Reverend Taplin wrote about this event in his diary.

Listen to Doreen. The recording was made some years ago and the quality is uneven. At one point in the story she uses an Aboriginal word which sounds like the English word 'melon' and means kill.

Did you find the false sentence?

B Proud to be an Aborigine

1 Another Aboriginal woman, Leila Rankine, gives her point of view about her people. What are her values? With a partner, choose appropriate words for the gaps before you listen. Think about the sort of views she might have before putting words in the spaces.

1 She doesn't want to be ....
2 She wants to prove her ....
3 She wants to share with and work for her ....
4 She loves ....
5 She wants to retain ....

Listen and then check your answers with others in the class.

2 Leila recites part of her poem called 'What it feels like to be black'. We hope you will enjoy the sincerity of her words.

3 **Extension** Write a few lines – or a poem, if you wish – about what it feels like to be you.

Key

Unit 1

A2 Speaker 1: f, a, c. Speaker 2: c, b. Speaker 3: e, a, d.

A3

	Jobs mentioned	*Reasons given for choosing them*
Speaker 1	television reporter, archaeologist, anthropologist	paid a lot of money, travel, see different countries, visit exciting places
Speaker 2	baseball player for New York Mets	best baseball team in the world
Speaker 3	photographer	work with people, be independent

B1 All three reasons are plausible, but (c) is probably the reason most British people would choose.

B2 Being unerringly pleasant, endlessly wonderful to people, having a certain height and perfect eyesight, perfectly turned out, having the right colour of nail varnish, being beautifully presented, elegant.

B3 psychiatric nurse

B4 b

Unit 2

A4 1 . . . he was first learning how to drive.
2 . . . lying down (sideways).
3 . . . he relaxed and the dog didn't bite.

A5 1 . . . starts whimpering and moving her legs frantically.
2 . . . run away.
3 . . . round her neck or attacking her knee.

B2 c, d

B4

	Where was she?	*What happened?*
Experience 1	on a tree	a cobra and a ratsnake fighting below, she was stuck to the tree
Experience 2	in a convent in the outskirts of city	she reached for a belt and it was a snake
Experience 3	in a temporary school building	snake fell on her head

Unit 3

A1 Rubik's cube, puzzle book, crossword puzzle, Scrabble, Chinese chequers, jigsaw puzzle, backgammon, Boggle.

A2

	Monopoly	Lateral thinking puzzles +		Jigsaw puzzles –	Backgammon	
Mah-jong						Boggle +
Chinese chequers		Trivial Pursuits +	Chess	Crosswords +		Scrabble +

A3 Speaker 1: Loves doing crosswords – she's a crossword freak. Loves all word games, anything like Scrabble and Boggle. Anything to do with words gives her a lot of pleasure.
Speaker 2: Likes puzzles – loves Trivial Pursuits, five years after it was invented.
Speaker 3: Can't stand puzzles. Jigsaw puzzles drive her insane. Does them with her children. But likes lateral thinking puzzles – not on paper. Likes being set a question and having to work it out – doesn't like organised puzzles.
Speaker 4: Asks about Boggle – a game with letters – you shake them and make words out of the way the letters land.

B2 sit

B3 abandon, alert, review

B4 up

B5 thinking

Unit 4

A2 Discontented shoppers: buy only what's on a list, are not relaxed (tense), are in a bad mood, don't like chatting, don't enjoy shopping or browsing or looking for bargains.

A3 The man on the tape: makes a list, goes through as quickly as possible, gets in a bad mood, doesn't like talking to people he meets (likes to shop on his own with nobody around), goes home and forgets about it.

A4 1 Yes 2 Yes 3 No 4 No 5 No 6 Yes 7 No

B3 magazine, book, newspaper, walkman, a cup of tea.

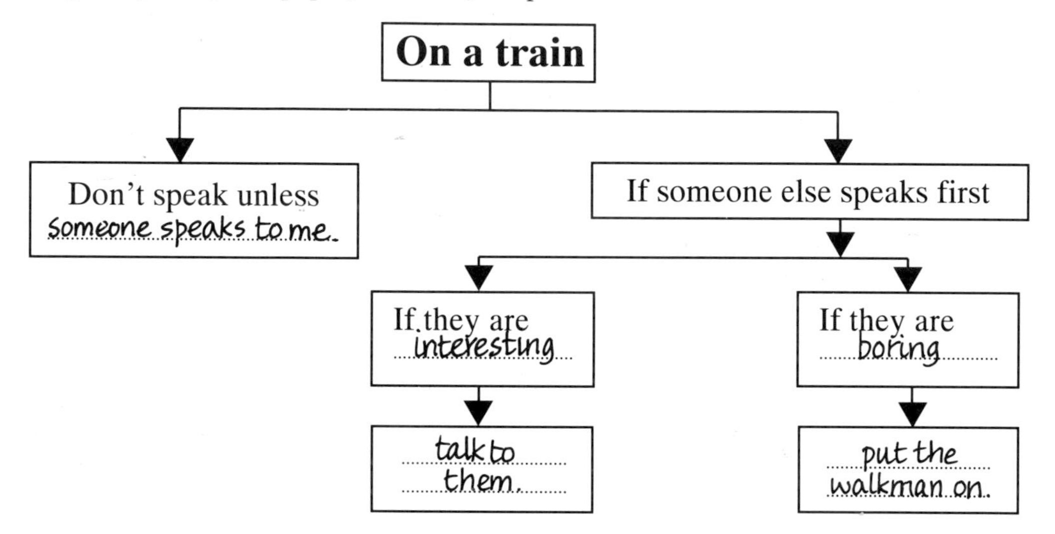

There are no right/wrong answers to the interpretation alternatives. They are designed to stimulate discussion.

Unit 5

A1 *God Save the Queen*, the national anthem of Britain.

A2 The similar statements are : 1 a, 2 a, 3 b.

A3 Speaker 1: (not) militaristic, represents a country, lyrical, hard, solemn, makes the people laugh, very rhythmic sound.
Speaker 2: very rousing, not a great song, old-fashioned, religious, royalist, a simple tune, it represents the sea and an island.
Speaker 3: long, different tunes and textures, seemed strange at first but later thought it splendid.

Unit 6

A2 He wonders if he is right to be interested, and about his morbid curiosity. He can stand outside and watch.

B3 Student A: Person killed: wife, Anna and daughter, Lupita.
Circumstances: shot dead as they slept.
Sentence: set free.
Student B: Person killed: son Carl.
Circumstances: smothered with a pillow. Mother unwell.
Sentence: sent to psychiatric hospital.

Student C: Victim: her lover, a milkman.
Circumstances: tried to choke him to death but went back to save cat.
Sentence: put on probation.

Unit 7

A2 Speaker 1: dancing, doing things you don't normally do, having fun, letting go, being primitive, having fun to different kinds of music.
Speaker 2: chatting to different people, everybody talking to everybody, meeting different people.

A3 a, d.

B3 It was the fortieth wedding anniversary of a deaf couple.
They felt the vibration of the music through the floorboards.
The deaf people made everyone feel at home and part of their group.

Unit 8

A2

Birthing centres	*Having a baby at home*	*Having a baby in hospital*
bedroom and kitchen like a home in the hospital near delivery suites safe	very small proportion risks involved chance of losing baby can be as safe little encouragement	more people involved chance of infection doctors prefer it

B2 She cut off the younger brother's curls because she was jealous of him.

B3 1T 2T 3F 4T 5F 6F 7F 8T

B4 Possible answers: 'I had a harder time than you two.' 'You got all the attention from our parents.' 'Mum and Dad were much more interested in you than in me.'

Unit 9

A1 1 Nelson Mandela 2 General de Gaulle 3 Charlie Chaplin 4 Marilyn Monroe 5 Dame Kiri Te Kanawa 6 Indira Gandhi

A3

Name	*Occupation*	*Where did speaker meet/ see him?*	*Speaker's reactions*
Gordon Banks	footballer (goalkeeper)	centre of Stoke-on-Trent/ speaker's home town	riveted to the spot, couldn't take my eyes off him, rooted to the spot, couldn't believe my luck, wonderful experience
Ray Davies	singer	in a cinema	a great moment, felt shy, wanted to tell him she liked his songs but couldn't

A4 Speaker 1: 'you know' 1; 'kind of' 0; 'sort of' 1.
Speaker 2: 'you know' 3; 'kind of' 2; 'sort of' 3.

B1 a) JH b) PN c) PN d) PN e) PN f) JH g) PN

B2 1 five foot 7½; 2 'Hey man, OK fine'; 'Hey man I don't play chords, I just play the sounds'; 'Feel it, experience yourself'.

Unit 10

B1 The town on the right bank thought that it was superior because it was the principal destination of the road. It thought the hole should be mended by the left bank town as it was of less consequence.

The town on the left bank thought that it was superior because all the traffic came to them. It thought the hole should be mended by the right bank town because it was in the interest of the right bank town to do so.

B2 1 broke his leg 2 the right bank 3 he was drunk that night.

B3 The correct order is: C, D, B, E, A.
1 angry 2 buy the hole 3 owned the hole 4 rushed to mend the hole 5 hole

C1

	Reactions
Speaker 1	Why is the ending violent? Interested in the story, in people in it, but violence negates the purpose of a story so reaction is negative.
Speaker 2	Doesn't know how true it would be, it suggests villagers are simpletons and traveller is cleverer.
Speaker 3	There isn't a moral to the story. The violence isn't a nice thing to end on.
Speaker 4	The way the traveller gets the hole filled in is funny. But why do they beat up all the travellers? Didn't understand the moral.

Unit 11

A2

	Problem	*What was done*
Speaker 1	teeth pointed in several directions, teeth now sliding back	lots of wire bands round her teeth, complicated, expensive dentistry
Speaker 2	bad teeth	false teeth at age 14
Speaker 3	two prominent front teeth	considerable work done to straighten them out

A3 Positive: peppermint taste, used the braces to show off at school.
Negative: jelly was like window putty, exploded in the mouth, other children made fun of people wearing braces, they were uncomfortable, painful, a constant pain.

B1 1 Percentages in Britain: 42%, 14%, 8%, 14%, 8%, 14%.
2 *definitely* percentage first, then *to some extent* i) 37%, 68% ii) 33%, 62% iii) 30%, 56% iv) 10%, 23% v) 6%, 19%
3 72% said yes.

(Statistics from *Adult Dental Health UK 1988*, Jean E. Todd and Deborah Lader, London, HMSO, 1991)

B3 I thought of something else, my toes turned up, my arms went rigid, my hands went white at the knuckles, I was being extremely brave, I had gas, I threw up, I passed out, I screamed.

Unit 12

A2 c, f

A3

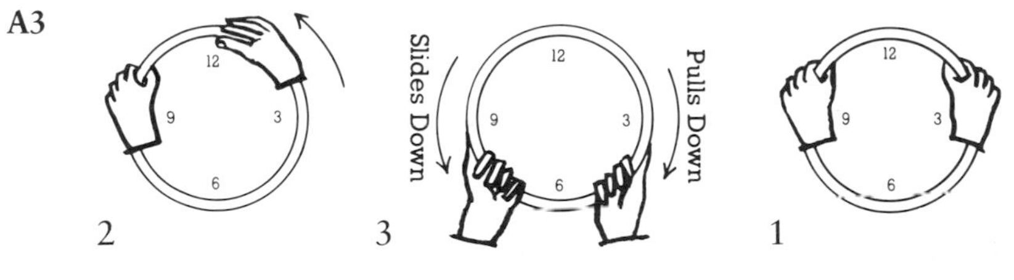

B2

	What they felt like when they started	*What they did first*
Speaker 1	it was exhilarating	sat down, wrote out everything known, then saw bank manager
Speaker 2	independent at last	filled in detailed questions in his business plan
Speaker 3	glad and worried	talked to friends, made notes which became business plan
Speaker 4	wondered why he hadn't done it before	made plan which made him see he needed a partner, wrote out a new plan for partner

B3 Sentences e, h and a describe how the problem happened. Sentences c, b, d, g and f describe what Alan did about it.

Unit 13

A2 Add up the numbers for the answers you gave.

1 yes 0; no 2   2 yes 0; no 2   3 yes 0; no 2   4 yes 0; no 2   5 yes 0; no 2
6 yes 0; no 2   7 yes 0; no 2   8 yes 1; no 2   9 yes 0; no 2   10 yes 0; no 2

Here are the profiles (what your score means):

If you scored between 11 and 20:
Your attitude towards crying is a healthy one. You aren't ashamed to let your emotions show occasionally, and you will undoubtedly be healthier because of this attitude.

If you scored between 6 and 10:
You know how to let your emotions show but still find it difficult. When you feel sad, let yourself cry. Allowing your emotions out in this way will do wonders for your physical and mental health.

If you scored 5 or less:
You need to cry openly and let your emotions show a little bit more. There really isn't anything wrong in letting people know how you feel. The more you struggle to restrain your natural impulses, the more likely it is that those impulses will damage your health.

A3 Speaker 1: at sad articles in newspapers, at my own life, at the life of my parents.
Speaker 2: I express myself easily, more so during bereavement.
Speaker 3: at a really sad film, at the birth of a baby.

A4 Speaker 1: It's an immense relief.
Great Britain would be a better place if people did vent their grief more openly – women live longer because they cry, men should cry more, it's a good thing to see a man crying.
Speaker 2: Laughing and expressing himself easily.
There were mourners, some paid, who wept and showed their emotions and let their joy and happiness for his father's life be visible.
If you don't grieve at a person's death, you carry your feelings about that person bottled up within you.
Speaker 3: When she did counselling training.
She had to be counselled herself.
She discovered all sorts of things that had been hidden, and was able to wipe the slate clean.

B2 a, b, f

B5 laughter

Unit 14

A2 In picture: waterproof suit, helmet, ropes, jamming device. Not in picture: light, Wellie boots.

A3 *It's safe:* Caving isn't dangerous compared with rugby football, trams or buses. It's unlikely that you're going to have an accident.

What do you mean, it's safe!!: You're hung by not very much over a big black hole. The consequences of having anything other than a very small accident are quite severe.

A4 July 22 entry: Spent night at top camp. . . . helped down hill. Put in car and taken to hospital in Oviedo.

August 26 entry: . . . so he moved back a bit and stone fell where his head had been.

B1 It takes about 16 hours to train.
The wingspan of an average glider is 18–20 metres.
They are made of fibreglass.
The trainee sits in front of the instructor.

B3
1 an average Boeing 727.
2 So that they don't worry and think he's gone to sleep.
3 It's like sitting in a comfortable chair on a scenic look-out.
4 In his seventies.
5 Over 90; a home-built aircraft.
6 Getting away from it all, it forces your mind off everything else.

Unit 15

B2 Possible questions:
2 How wide was the footpath?
3 How far could you see down? *or* How high up were you?
4 What did you dream about that night?
5 Where did you spend the night?
6 What was the weather like the following morning?
7 How did you get down the mountain?

Unit 16

A2 Speaker 1: for airline tickets.
Speaker 2: to buy petrol, to get cash quickly, to open locked doors.
Speaker 3: to keep monthly accounts.

A4 Speaker 1: 1 (she 'watches' her cards) but she disregards 4.
Speaker 2: 1, 4, 5.

B2 e, b, g, d, c, a, f. She was alarmed because they withdrew more money than she had in her account.

B3 1b 2c 3a

Unit 17

A2 His wife, because he can discuss anything with her, and she intuitively knows how he is feeling even if he doesn't show it.

B1 The friend was jealous of Maggie, and wanted everything she had.

B2 Other possible mottos include: Friendship is trust, Friends like each other even when they make mistakes, Friends are your other memory, Friendship is a lot of common knowledge, Friends have so much in common.

Unit 18

A1 Ireland, Puerto Rico, Nigeria, Bangladesh, Malaysia, New Zealand.

A2
1 The main language I learned was English.
2 I was born in a poor area of Glasgow.
3 When I speak Glaswegian nobody understands a word I say.
4 When I went to drama school they laughed at me.
5 Glaswegian has dialect words like 'mines' for 'mine' and 'but' at the end of a sentence.

A3
1 An Irishman will never use one word when he can use ten.
2 Irish people say: Hang on a second I'll be back in a minute.
3 Irish people say: It's great to see you and when are you going home?
4 The Irish and the Scots are very poetic.
5 When I came to England I had a strong Indian accent.
6 I didn't think much about it but the other kids laughed.
7 I noticed that kids in the class with high marks spoke the Queen's English.

8 People said to me: have you got a cold?
9 Well I never got high marks but people stopped laughing at me.

B2 Speaker 1: French and Spanish. English. Nepalese – by playing with the servants – just picked it up.
Speaker 2: English, French, German, Italian – not from a book, just living in the countries – through necessity.

B3 – learning Latin, learning Italian.
– English or Scottish teacher teaching French, Italian schoolteacher.
– French, Latin, Italian.

Unit 19

A2
1 everything about her.
2 what her parents would think about the marriage.
3 why her son couldn't find a nice Russian girl.
4 wouldn't be able to understand her son.

A3 The main issues were that the daughter-in-law was foreign and coloured. The daughter-in-law was upset at the way people looked at her. The mother-in-law eventually accepted her and wanted to be friends. She came to feel her daughter-in-law was like everybody else, although she still referred to other people as foreign.

A4 People have the best of both worlds, people are able to visit and understand others; prejudice is reduced if people are known personally.

B2 Holland, America, Switzerland, Australia, Britain.

They keep in contact by visiting cousins, meeting once a week, weddings.

B3 At first he felt strange, he didn't like it much, but now he feels it's an excuse for his family to visit.

Although his grandmother speaks American English, she finds it difficult to understand British English. She has difficulties with the currency, and with public transport (in Texas she drives her own car). She can't drive in England because she wouldn't be used to driving on the left.

Unit 20

A1 1b 2c 3c 4b 5c 6c

A2
1 She has nine children.
2 She has been foster mother to 23 children.
3 She has 20 grandchildren.

A3
1 a death
2 broken marriages
3 better than white foster homes

A4 3 is false. He chose not Jane but his older wife who already had children.

B1
1 She doesn't want to be isolated.
2 She wants to prove her capabilities.
3 She wants to share with and work for her community.
4 She loves stories, poems, music, young people.
5 She wants to retain cultural ties and links.

Tapescript

Unit 1 Jobs, desirable and undesirable

1A Jobs: My idea of hell, my idea of heaven

EXERCISE 2

I think my idea of hell would be, to be, to have a job where I had to do the same thing over and over again like somebody working in a factory just picking up one thing from one place and putting it into another and this just going on and on, day in and day out, if it was that kind of job I would just go mad . . .

Well, I think the thing I would least like to do given an option of anything in the world would be to be the guy who sits in a nuclear power station watching for it to start melting down, you know, the guys who sit there in front of those, that's just you know it's a revolting thing anyway but can you imagine the boredom and the responsibility at the same time, it would just be completely terrible, I'd hate that.

I think I think the job I I don't actually think I would be capable of doing it is to be work as the killing person in an abattoir. I think that would be my my er it's self-explanatory why I couldn't do it. I th . . . I can't imagine how people actually do it. I met somebody once who erm was one of the people that went into erm er a chicken battery and they'd spend all night they were only working night shift and just kill chickens and and I just couldn't comprehend how they managed to do that and how they stayed sane. That would be the worst thing. I think it'd be torture in more ways than one . . .

EXERCISE 3

On the other hand it would be wonderful to have a job where you are paid a lot of money and you could travel to different countries – someone like a television reporter or an archaeologist or an anthropologist. I mean those are the exciting kinds of jobs I'd like to have . . . I can't pinpoint one but it has to be a job where I can travel and see different countries and have time to actually stay in those countries and learn a little about those countries and visit exciting places.

What would I like to do? Well I guess probably the best job in the world would be to play for the New York Mets. You can't beat that . . . you just can't beat that . . . third base man for the New York Mets. The Mets? Oh they're a baseball team . . . best baseball team in the world.

To choose another sort of job that I would really like. I would very much like to be a photographer, erm because it would give me an opportunity to work with people but at the same time be independent still and that's the thing that I always need. I need to be independent, be able to work on my own and be amongst other people, very much like you, I think, that I have to have other contact but like to get on with wha . . . with my own thing.

1B Have you got what it takes to be a . . .?

EXERCISE 2

I longed to be an air hostess . . . until I discovered that planes crashed (*laughter*) and then I decided I decided I'd be an air hostess who worked on the ground . . . I think this er . . . I don't know how long I wanted to be an air hostess for I don't actually think I could be now . . . unerringly pleasant on a long journey (*didn't you have . . .*) endlessly wonderful to people who might be snotty and horrible (*didn't you have to be a certain height as well?*) yes and I wasn't that and er they asked for perfect eyesight then when I was little (*did they?*) and I had glasses, you had to be perfectly turned out and there in those days was a set of rules about the colour of the nail varnish you had and this and that and the other and they were always so beautifully presented, they were so elegant and they went all over the world that I thought that this was the height of glamour to be an air hostess. (*now they're flight attendants*) Now they're flight attendants not even stewards or stewardesses, now they're flight attendants still looking beautifully turned out.

EXERCISE 4

. . . You have to be of a fairly strong disposition somehow (*mm*) to be a psychiatric nurse (*absolutely*) as a friend did become one but she couldn't make the difference, the change in her own mind between over-empathetic and sympathetic as a nurse in being becoming over-empathetic and feeling with these people that she actually lost her own sense of identity (*mm*) and she ended up having a nervous breakdown, she just couldn't make that change (*it does drive you crazy*) she in fact actually stopped being a good nurse because she was feeling too much for the patients and the type of treatments and things that were there. So I think you have to be a very very special type of person. (*I think that's why I couldn't do it on a full-time basis*)

Unit 2 A bit of a nightmare

2A Bad dreams

EXERCISE 4

Well I never really had a lot of nightmares or anything but I did I did have one this morning . . . erm. I don't know when I don't know if it was just as I was waking up or just you know but I remembered it very vividly when I woke up and it's just a little like an image of of I was lying sideways, in a car . . . you know just with the the and I remember the car, it was the car that that I had when I was first learning how to drive and I was lying sideways in this car and I think it was just as I was lying down, and as I lay down I put my . . . shoulder my neck that that really sensitive section right there . . . and and I lay down right into a Dobermann's mouth and he started to bite and then I started to relax and as I relaxed he didn't bite . . . so the more I relaxed the less he bit. I don't know if I was just tense . . .

EXERCISE 5

I seem to have a recurring nightmare erm . . . starts of course . . . my husband waking me quickly because I start whimpering and moving my legs frantically because I'm trying to run away, and I'm trying to run away from wretched snakes . . . and these snakes are always either round my neck or attacking my knee of all places.

2B What do dreams mean?

EXERCISE 2

– . . . I don't know if I was just tense when I was sleeping or what but it really it was a very vivid image of this. I've never been bitten by a dog.
– Did you feel pain? Did you wake up with (*no*) aware of pain?
– No, I just woke up aware of, boy that was weird wasn't it, you know it was that kind of a thing.
– You hadn't got physical sensations?
– No . . .
– Were you . . . this was this morning (*this morning*) you obviously expected this session in the studio to be so painful (*laughter and several people trying to speak*) and decided when it gets really difficult and they're screaming at me from the other side of the glass, they're recording this programme, I must relax (*maybe that's it, maybe that's it, I'll buy that*).

EXERCISE 4

– Now a lot of people will say, 'Oh dear this is something very significant . . . her dreaming of snakes' but it's nothing to do with any kind of erm . . . double meaning that there may be. It's because as a child, I lived in the East and I had many nasty experiences with snakes. Once I was up on a tree . . . I was a very little girl and down below a cobra and a ratsnake, they actually were fighting, and they fought to the death and I used to put my arms round the tree and I was just stuck there and then after everything was finished, they had to send some people up the tree to prise my arms open and bring me down again. And another time we had just moved from one convent which was in a sort of a . . . fairly civilised part of the city to the outskirts and I reached out to get what I thought was a belt hanging up and of course it was a

wretched snake. (*terrible*) Then we had patched roofs in some of the temporary school buildings and snakes liked to go up onto this roof. And I happened to be standing talking to a nun, and you know how in the course of conversation you tend to change places (*mm*) and we had just changed places when this wretched snake fell on my head and I went into hysterics . . . and I just can't seem to get over this fear and I have this recurring nightmare . . .
- Is it always the same, is it . . . are you always in the same place and the same snakes and . . .
- No, different places and they're always so colourful and they always try to get my neck, round my neck or they try to get my knee and it's . . .
- Whereabouts as a matter of interest, whereabouts was this, when you were a child?
- This was in Sri Lanka. (*Sri Lanka*) Yes (*good heavens . . . extraordinary*) and as a result, I can be offered work if there's anything to do with snakes I will just say no, I can't . . . you can offer me a million pounds and I will not do it. I can't bear to see the picture of a snake on the screen or in a magazine. I can be all alone but I go into hysterics.

Unit 3 Puzzles

3A I love puzzles and games

EXERCISES 2 AND 3

- I love doing crosswords, I'm a real crossword freak. Erm, I love, I love all word games, you know, anything like Scrabble and Boggle and all those kinds of things. Erm, and er, anything really to do with words gives me a lot of pleasure, yes.
- Yeah, I like puzzles in general. I love Trivial Pursuits, I'm afraid, I know it's, I know it's a bit passé now, sort of five, five years after it was invented, but I do love playing things like Trivial Pursuit, and I love puzzles in general.
- Am, I can't stand puzzles basically because jigsaw puzzles drive me insane. But I do them with my children. Erm . . . but really I, I like lateral thinking puzzles which aren't actually you know on paper. I like being set a question and having to work it out. But otherwise I don't like organised puzzles.
- Mm, yeah, Juliet, what's Boggle? (*laughter*)
- Scrabble and Boggle . . . What's Boggle?
- Boggle, it's a cube filled with letters, you shake it, the letters all land in a configuration, and you have to make words out of the way the letters land.
- Oh, I see. it's called Boggle.

3B Thinking it out

EXERCISE 2

- Right, come on, let's get down to this crossword.
- Three across: what do you say to your dog when he is too frisky – three, three letters. (*mm mm*) O that's difficult . . .
- Oh, we know that one . . .
- Sit!
- Sit. All right, let's write that one in. (*all right*)
- Sit.
- Now are we going to go through it methodically or (*yes*) are we going to go . . . All right, OK.

EXERCISE 3

- Well, let's go on to the next one, six across. Leave all behind. Seven letters. (*several together: leave all behind . . . leave all behind*)
- Leave all behind . . .
- Abandon, A, abandon.
- A-B A-(*others join in*) N-D-O-N. Could be (*Could be – all talk together*) . . .
- Well, let's have a look, let's have a look what six down is. 'Cause if six down begins with A . . . (*Yes*) Fully awake and attentive and get others to be the same.
- Alert.
- Yeah.
- But why get others to be the same?
- When you're on alert . . . (*Oh, yeah . . . Mm . . . Yeah*)
- Got to be, hasn't it?
- Right, OK, so, er . . .
- Let's put that in . . . alert.
- Alert, A-L-E-R-T . . . (*Six down*) right . . .
- An . . . don . . . We're not doing too badly, are we . . .
- Very good, and I haven't said a thing! (*laughter*)
- All right, now seven across, criticise, then have a second look.
- Ah, I know what that is . . . (*Oh . . . Clever*

clogs) Review. Review. Re-view. (*Oh yes, very clever.*)
- Oh, I got you, view like second (*Yes . . . and criticise as well*) look, I see, second . . .
- I before E . . .
- Except after C.
- Right. Good.
- If the sound is E . . . (*Oh, Ooh, Booh . . .*)
- I'm better at music than at crosswords. (*laughter*)

EXERCISE 5

- What about one down? That looks a very difficult one.
- Well, let me do that one. (*laughter*) That's one letter . . . Where things go before they come down . . . right. Where things go before they come down. (*laughter*) I think that's up.
- OK. Right, a concerted effort now, there's one more to get, it's four down.
- The longest.
- What you are doing now but can your dog do it as well?
- What . . . what are we doing now?
- We're . . . terminating?
- We're turning, we're . . . it's got to be N something I-N-G.
- Yes. N-T-I-N-G? N . . .
- Thinking?
- (*yes, well done*)

Unit 4 How do you . . .?

4A . . . do the shopping?

EXERCISE 3

Well basically what I do is always make up a list, because I tend to forget the very thing that I've gone to shop for when I've arrived there and it's quite simple. I go into the supermarket because I don't like shopping at all and I go through as quickly as possible without any interference from anybody that I might meet 'cause I generally meet the whole world in the supermarket and I pay up as quickly as possible, I put it in the car, and I'm home. That's as basic as I can get about shopping, erm, the journey there is always something . . . I tend to get in a bad mood just before I go and when I'm coming home I'm in a bad mood, so I like to shop on my own with nobody around so it's as simple as that with me, er, shopping is, er, an arduous activity and everything is just listed plain and simple and bye bye forget it.

EXERCISE 4

I have to say that I do my shopping in completely the opposite way to you because, mind you the only similarity is that I can't stand anyone there or if I have to take one of the children they have to sit in one in you know those seats (*the trolleys*) they have to sit in them and they're not allowed out because otherwise I mean people who take children shopping, it's a nightmare, you spend your life running after them and putting things back on the shelves that they've grabbed, but I go in one door and I go up one aisle. I don't eat meat so I don't bother with that. I go up one aisle and I take the things off there, I always know what I want I go down the next one, up down up and down and then I go back to the frozen food and I put that on the top and then if I have to queue I start I'm almost like I'm driving because I think . . . why do they sell frozen food and then make me queue while it defrosts and I kind of swear to myself . . .

But the worst thing for me about shopping is when I get it home because then there's no one to help you so I get the wheelbarrow then and 'cause I live in the country, you see, and I fill up the wheelbarrow with boxes and erm it's quite bumpy where I live and I go over the bumps and boxes fall off and things fall out and by the end of it what started out as a very organised sort of activity ends up with me in a really bad mood.

4B . . . cope with a long journey?

EXERCISE 3

- If I go on a journey, er, let's say a two-hour train journey, I actually dislike travelling, er, in that sense, er, so I always try and take a particular magazine and, er, a book and a newspaper and my walkman. And I try and erm, read for fifteen minutes and listen to the walkman for fifteen minutes, then get up and go and buy a cup of tea. I try and sort of carve, er, er, have various things to do throughout the two hours so that two hours doesn't seem as long and boring as as, er, it can often be. And, you know, that's how I deal with travelling.
- What about crossword puzzles?
- No, I don't, I don't really bother with crossword puzzles.
- What about engaging in conversations with people?
- I enjoy, well I think this might be another

English thing. I don't do it, I just don't do it. Partly because I think it's, I think that they might think I'm just taking liberties in talking to them. (*ah, I see*) But having said that, if somebody starts to talk to me, (*yeah*) if they're interesting, then, um, I'll talk to them. If they're boring that walkman goes on. (*I see . . . don't invade my space*) Absolutely. Absolutely.

Unit 5 National anthems

5A A rousing tune

EXERCISES 2 AND 3

– Well, really, all I, I can really say is that, er, our music really reflects the people in our country. So, when I hear my national anthem I always want to stand up and sing out as loud as possible. Now, a lot of Europeans always sort of say that music is very militaristic, but it is not. It represents an emerging African country, after years and years of sort of colonial rule . . . Our song is 'Stand up and fight for a land . . .' so you have to stand there . . . So it is lyrical, it is hard, it is solemn . . . so it makes us laugh as well. Really. And one thing I learnt when I was at school was that every time before class started, we would have to stand up and sing the song. The words I always forgot, but the music stayed inside of me. And it also had a very rhythmic sound to it. So it was militaristic, yes, but it never forgot the music coming from the people.
– Well, I have to say that almost in spite of myself I find my national anthem very rousing and when I hear it, even though it . . . in a way it's not . . . it's not a great song at all, I, I find the hairs on the back of my neck start, start jumping up . . . and, erm and I do feel a kind of fervour and pride about my country, erm, even though it's a, it's a very old-fashioned song, erm . . . it's, it's, it's, it's a, it's a religious song, it's a, it's a very, um . . . royalist song . . . erm . . . and, and, and yet for some reason it does, it does have this effect on me . . . erm . . . it's, it's a simple tune, you know, most people could pick it up very quickly and I think the thing that really gets you is that in the middle there's this, there's this sort of scale that goes up and it's, and it's sort of getting you going, charging up towards mountains and and or or into the sea, because it also sort of represents an island.
– Can you sing it for us, Juliet?
– I, I could do, I . . .
– Yeah . . .
– The thing is, though, you see, I don't know the words.
– I always forget the words as well . . .
– I know, it's like you know the first two lines of of, of, of an anthem and then you just, the rest of it goes out the window but I could sing you the first two lines anyway so it goes: God save our gracious Queen, Long live our noble Queen, God save our Queen . . . Da da da da . . . Long to . . . and it's that bit, you see.
– That's very similar to ours – ba da ba ba ba, Stand up and fight . . .
– Well, I was brought up in a colonial country, where we had the national anthem of the colonial power and because I was so used to that as a national anthem, when this country gained its independence and they had, a . . . different national anthem, which for one thing went on for, it just went on and on and on, and because I wasn't used to the fact that this had all sorts of different kinds of tunes and textures, it was strange to me and I couldn't think of it as a national anthem. But once I got used to it and learnt it then I thought it was splendid.

5B Editing a radio programme

EXERCISES 1 and 3

Conversation 1

– Well my national anthem is . . . it leaves me cold, really . . . er . . . I have to say . . . er for most purposes, except er, at major sporting events or something like that where your country wins the gold medal (*laughter*) and they hoist the flag in the middle and the other countries, the second and third, are slightly lower than your flag (*laughter*) and you hear your national anthem beating out and you feel, you do feel very, very proud. But, erm, I, I feel it's a sort of, it's a bit of a psychological trick really. I mean, it does, like you said, Juliet, it gets the blood flowing and, and you do feel great but, er, I have to say in the cold light of day if I think about my national anthem it, it, I feel it's jingoistic and you know, it's a bit, bit, a bit of a con, really.

And I feel that about national anthems in general . . . erm . . . so for me fine at sporting events but, you know, best . . .
– Don't you think the world is a different place, though, than it was when when we all . . .
– Absolutely, I absolutely do, erm . . . maybe, well we're in the nineties now, but maybe, certainly just after the War, you know, perhaps during the fifties . . . national pride was er . . . a really big thing. Well I think it is still to an extent with, with many people but there is er, there's a whole sort of section of society now who, who reject the idea of these sort of, these militaristic anthems and songs . . .
– And you agree with certain sentiments of that?
– Oh sure, yeah. But, erm . . . It . . . it would be nice if there was a world anthem.
– A world anthem. A peace anthem.
– Yeah, exactly.
– That's what we need.
– Exactly.
– Well, all right, OK.

Conversation 2
– To me it's, it's different, different than that. Now to me, it's, it's sports. Before the game, you know. (*yeah?*) Yeah. Yeah, everybody stands, and you put your, your baseball cap or your hand over your heart and, and I suppose it is a bit solemn, but I guess to me, maybe it's just the connection with being a kid and being in the, you know in the ball park and, you know, it's not really a solemn thing, it's just the . . . thing that you do, you know, before you can play baseball . . .
– Now I actually hate national anthems being sung (*do you*) because I think it's dreadful. I feel that nations should be getting closer together, and a national anthem is something which says, 'Oh, my country's (*my country's better, my country's . . . yeah*) more important than yours, my song is better than yours (*yeah*) and therefore I'm not actually in favour of national anthems any more . . .
– No I see why, but I think, I don't know, I think it's kind of a . . . you know, an unrealistic expectation that people aren't going to be competitive with their . . . their national I mean, look at the Olympics and the whole, you know (*mm*) . . . the . . .
– But that's the point. At the Olympics, when the flag of the country goes up, and this anthem comes, (*yeah*) is played, you think, 'Oh my god, yet again!' (*laughter*)
– Well, I guess it depends if it's your country or not . . .
– It takes away from the achievement of that particular winner (*mm*) and they talk about the country. And it's that . . .
– Maybe you're right.
– particular person's achievement.

Unit 6 Crime and punishment

6A A morbid interest?

EXERCISE 2

Well, I have to confess that I'm very taken by the sort of television programme which I saw last week and which shows how, er, the police go about, er trying to find criminals. The programme that I saw was about a rapist, erm, and the police were able to find out tiny bits of information erm, clues, that he'd left like bits of, er, paint that his car left on the, on the branch of a tree, and, er, and he buried, er, a rifle somewhere and all manner of tiny, tiny little clues and it's actually the subject of rape is is, erm, a very emotive one, but this programme was very cold and calculated and I had to admit it was, it was fascinating, it really was. And er, I, I, I sometimes wonder whether I'm right to be interested in, in that sort of television programme. I have to also admit that when they deal with the subject of murder, there is definitely a morbid curiosity within me. I don't know if you feel that, but there's something that . . . because you can stand outside somehow and watch, er, a murder investigation, there's something, it's just, I don't know, it's just a morbid curiosity that I do find fascinating, you know? And I guess that's why films, you know, feature films about murder erm are so, are so popular.

6B Make the punishment fit the crime

EXERCISE 4

1 Protests over the freeing of an army captain who killed his wife and baby daughter raged on today, with calls for the resignation of the judge who told the man, 'You have my deep sympathy'. A jury at the High Court found Captain John Dulaita guilty of killing his wife Anna, aged 24, and their two-year-old

daughter Lupita. The captain shot them dead as they slept in their apartment last February, then telephoned the police to give himself up. The judge, Lord Mathias, told him, 'In my opinion you have punished yourself more than enough by what you did. You will have to live with this for the rest of your life.' But today it was revealed that the court had been inundated with protests. The secretary of the local branch of the action group Victim Support said the decision was completely unacceptable: 'Whether or not it was deliberate, the fact is that two lives were taken. And this decision by the judge . . . is . . . well, it's an absolute disgrace.' The MP for the region said that the matter would be referred to a special committee.

2 A mother who killed her child after being left brain-damaged by surgery was put on probation for three years today at the High Court in Aberdeen. Martha Rudven smothered 16-month-old Carl with a pillow, then swallowed pills and slashed one of her wrists, but she was found by a neighbour and rushed to hospital. Ten months ago she was diagnosed as having a brain tumour and had life-saving surgery which left her with serious disabilities. She decided to kill herself and the baby when she became depressed at her lack of progress after the operation. Judge John Erickson told her, 'It is not my wish to punish you, but to help you. You were the most loving and caring of mothers and I have no doubt this whole tragic case arose from an accident of fortune.' The jury agreed that the killing had been the result of the tumour and the operation. Mrs Rudven who admitted manslaughter was referred to a psychiatric hospital for treatment.

3 A woman who started a bedroom fire to kill her lover was put on probation for two years after admitting arson. The judge heard that Gretta Lanski had set fire to clothes near her sleeping lover with the intention that he should choke to death in the smoke. Then she had second thoughts when she realised her cat might also be trapped. In court, Mrs Lanski claimed that her lover, a milkman, was violent and had beaten her several times in the past. The judge told her, 'I can see no sign of remorse for this serious act which could well have cost a man's life. You only went back into the bedroom to fetch your cat and it was only after the man woke up that you called the fire brigade.'

However, the judge added that there would be little benefit in sending her to prison as she had now broken with the man and was unlikely to be in a position to repeat her violent act.

Unit 7 Memorable parties

7A *What I enjoy most about parties is . . .*

EXERCISE 2

– I find parties are really a chance above all else to just perhaps do the things you can't do on an everyday basis in most er social situations, erm, by which I mean really to have fun and dance and let yourself go a bit and, erm, maybe be a little bit more, erm what might be considered primitive . . . dancing and letting go and having fun to a range of different sort of music to me is an absolutely essential quality of a good party.

– But isn't that because you like dancing? (*Oh yes*) There are lots of people who enjoy parties but who can't dance (*Indeed, yes*) . . . erm . . . now what I like about a party is that you're going to meet . . . when you go to the party . you don't know most of the people there . . . usually you don't know most of the people there. But by the end of the evening if you could have chatted even for a few minutes to different people then I feel that . . . you know . . . I've enjoyed the party (*mm*) and I hate parties where erm . . . you only talk to one person or two people and you're stuck with them for the whole evening. For me a party is everybody's talking to everybody and . . . you know . . . erm . . . just having a marvellous time . . . meeting different people.

EXERCISE 3

– So many of us are very constrained by certain social . . . conformities and stuff so we desperately need to have parties or other structures where we can say for this two hours we can let go of it (*absolutely let rip*) (*yeah but don't you think it's . . .*) That may not mean smashing windows and being antisocial it may mean just experiencing

myself in a way that isn't necessarily as organised and disciplined and responsible as one has to be on a daily level. (*right . . . right*) You can say right, blow, let's go.
– Well I find what . . . what . . . up . . . upsets me about that is that so many people feel that they need to be drunk in order to reach that point (*that . . . that . . .*) I mean . . . I like . . . I like a drink as . . . as . . . as much as anybody else but . . . but there seems to be, you know, oh we have to get drunk to have a good time (*noisy interruptions from other speakers*) that has a lot to answer for . . .
– Oh I agree with you because it really doesn't . . . you don't need liquor to have a nice time and so often don't you find that . . . erm . . . you've actually sometimes thought . . . Oh, I don't want to go to that party today and then that particular party, which you didn't want to go to, has given you the greatest pleasure. (*yeah . . . yeah*)

7B What a party!

EXERCISE 2

Erm . . . well . . . the most memorable party experience I had is one of intense embarrassment. I was invited to a party through a third party, through a friend, and erm I was told that it was fancy dress . . . and so I quite enjoy doing fancy dress . . . and . . . erm made quite a lot of effort . . . and . . . erm . . . went as this . . . in a very, very sort of elaborate witch costume . . . and . . . I arrived, terribly proud of myself . . . erm sort of at the right time, you know, not too early, not too late, to make an entrance, and in fact when I arrived at this party this friend had been pulling my leg, and I was the only person (*oh no*), amongst sixty people, who were casually dressed in jeans and sweaters, in fancy dress . . . I was appalled, I mean I should have had more bravado and sort of carried it off. (*Was that one of your best friends?*) . . . not a friend at all any more . . . erm . . . so I had to sort of, I prevailed upon the host, and said that she had to lend me something casual to dress in and I was I was actually really angry for some reason my sense of humour deserted me . . . and I felt terribly terribly exposed . . .

EXERCISE 3

I must tell you about the most fascinating party I've ever been to in my whole life. It was the fortieth wedding anniversary of a deaf couple, but this party was half deaf people, half hearing people, but you wouldn't have known the difference. Somehow, they made us all hearing people, part of this deaf evening . . . and they were dancing . . . at first I thought, my God, they're dancing . . . all the deaf people, but they were dancing beautifully . . . and . . . because they could actually hear the vibration through the floorboards. (*yes*) But what was wonderful about this party was that they made everyone feel at home and part of their group and it was for me it was the most exciting party I've ever been to in my life.

EXERCISE 4

There's a lovely story which is absolutely true. One of my best friends who as I said before is in the theatre business, in fact he's an entertainer, he . . . er . . . went to a party . . . he . . . on a Thursday night with a bottle of champagne and may I now add that he doesn't drink at all now, but in those days he used to drink quite heavily. And he knocked on the door of the house that he was invited to, a rather grand house, and the lady of the house came down after about five minutes in a dressing gown with a towel round her hair, and he said, 'Oh . . . ah . . . I've come for the party' and she said, 'There's not a party tonight, that was last Thursday, and you were there!' (*laughter*) . . . That's absolutely a true story.

Unit 8 Babies, brothers and sisters

8A Where were you born?

EXERCISE 2

– What about . . . erm . . . the number of mothers who are now choosing to have their babies at home. Is that a, a growing number in Australia?
– It's still a very very small proportion at the moment and therefore many, erm, hospitals are thinking of actually introducing birthing centres, birthing units, we have one at our hospital at the moment, where the, the unit is set up as a bedroom and a kitchen and the woman can actually walk around in comfort and just pretend it's her own home.
– So it's like a home in the hospital?
– Yeah, it's like a little maisonette in the hospital and, er, it's so close by to the theatre

and delivery suites that if anything should go wrong and did go wrong they could be moved around quite quickly and safely.
- Margaret, do you think it's safe to have a baby at home?
- There are risks involved, erm, I personally would prefer not to have my baby at home I mean it would be (*well you're a midwife*) I know it would be quite ideal but the risk of something going wrong and if I was to lose that baby I think that I would be quite devastated.
- Aren't there dangers in hospital because there are more people involved?
- There are dangers in hospital, I mean you you wouldn't want to know that there is a particularly resistant staphylococcal infection running around the hospital and, er, that would be quite a risk. In some countries it's been proven that having the baby at home is as safe as having a baby in hospital.
- Does it get a lot of encouragement having, er, a baby at home?
- I don't think so, no, it doesn't, I think erm doctors and I think mainly doctors probably I think they scare the women saying well this might go wrong or that might go wrong at home so it's better for you to come into hospital.

EXERCISE 3

Speaker 1

And erm I was going to have the baby at home and then two weeks before, a friend of mine erm had a baby that died . . . not at home or anything but it shocked me so I thought I'll go into hospital, and erm then I, I went into the hospital and four hours later there was this baby and it's a sort of such a surprise and and it was all wonderful and and I remember and it was huge it was huge great big baby and bouncy and fat and everything and and after two days erm they took her to a special care unit 'cause they thought she was convulsing and that was that was the most awful thing in my life and I remember now I look back and I remember something that one of my mother's friends said to her and she said you won't really know pain or worry or suffering until you have children, and that is really true, because worrying about yourself isn't isn't anything but as soon as you have children those worries are just huge in fact it was all erm it it was nothing there was nothing wrong with her and it it was a false alarm but in in a different way it changed my life.

Speaker 2

My wife and I came to a decision that we wanted a child at home so that we can remove any outside interference from the medical authorities. Well, we were lucky in the sense that there were no complications during the pregnancy and we were being supervised by a wonderful assortment of multinational midwives who came from Ireland, Jamaica, Nigeria, er, even Latin America, er, so during the nine-month period for the second birth of the child, we had got together a great team of, er, of women and I was like the token woman in the group and I was going against my own sort of culture where the father stayed at home and left it to the women. I wanted to be involved and the whole experience left me with one about my sheer admiration for the midwives, for the doctor who came in at the last moment and for my first daughter who was involved with the pregnancy as the baby grew.

8B Brothers and sisters

EXERCISE 2

- Well, my brother was six years younger than I, and er, I think that when he was little I was quite jealous of him. I remember he had beautiful red curls (*mm*) . . . my mother used to coo over him. One day a friend and I played, erm, barber shop, and, erm, my mother must have been away, she must have been in the kitchen or something (*mm*) and we got these scissors and sat my brother down and kept him quiet and (*strapped him down*) . . . That's right, and cut off all his curls, you see. And my mother just was so upset, and in fact it's the first . . . I think it's one of the few times I've ever seen my father really angry.
- What happened to you?
- Oh . . . I was sent to my room for a whole week you know, it was terrible.
- But was that the sort of pattern, weren't you close to your brother at all?
- Well as I grew older I think that er I just ignored him . . .

EXERCISE 3

- What about . . . you've got an older brother

too, did . . . were they close, the two brothers?

– No, no my brother's just a couple of years older than I so the two of us were closer and we thought we were both very grown up and he was just a . . . a kid so we deliberately, I think, kind of ignored him. And then I left, I left home when he was only still a schoolboy, he was only fifteen (*mm*) and I went to live in England and he eventually went to live in Brazil and I really did lose contact with him for a long time.
– What was he doing down there?
– Well, he was a travel agent, so he went down there to work . . . And, erm, I didn't, I can't even remember, erm sending a card, even, when he got married. But I re . . . I do remember that later on my mother was showing me pictures of his wedding, cause my mother and father went down there (*uh huh*) to the wedding, and er, there was this guy on the photos with a beard and glasses, and I said, 'Oh, who's this then?' 'cause I thought it was the bride's brother or something like this (*mm*) . . . and my mother said frostily, 'That . . . is your brother!' (*laughter*)

EXERCISE 4

– What, er, did he try to get in touch with you while you were living in different countries?
– N . . . no, no, we just had a total . . . really a total breakdown of communication. But just recently I've got together with him again, because I had to go down to Brazil for business (*mm*) and we we got together again and we got on very well. But the funny thing is that we have totally different recollections of our childhood. (*mm*) Because I remember him getting all the attention (*yeah*) but he thinks that he was a very neglected child and that our parents really were much more interested in the two elder children. I think children always have these feelings about their brothers or sisters, that they're always jealous. Wherever you are in the family. Like my older brother thinks that he had a much harder time than the two younger ones, because he feels that my father especially was much stricter with him because he was (*oh yeah*) expected to behave (*mm*) and to give an example, and so on.

Unit 9 Brief encounters

9A I couldn't take my eyes off him

EXERCISES 3 AND 4

Speaker 1

Well, living in London erm you often meet, er, or see well-known people on the Tube and, er, in the street and as an adult I must say it's, it's, no great thing . . . I . . . I hardly sort of turn a hair when I see someone well-known, but wh . . . I have a very vivid memory of about . . . when I was about twelve years old, I'm from Stoke-on-Trent and, er, I used to go and see my local team Stoke City play every two weeks at home and, er, I was walking through the town centre one day and I saw Gordon Banks. (*Ah . . . Gordon . . . the goalkeeper*) Absolutely. (*I hated him*) I was . . . well I was . . . I couldn't believe that I was seeing this idol of mine in the flesh, else, you know, somewhere else other than on the football field and I was just riveted to the spot, and I just couldn't take my eyes off him . . . he was just shopping . . . was browsing looking in a camera shop and erm but I just . . . was absolutely rooted to the spot and I watched him for ages and ages and I just couldn't believe my luck and that was the most wonderful experience and it's never been repeated since, 'cause you very soon grow up and become very hackneyed and cynical (*yes*) so, but I'll always have that memory.

Speaker 2

Well, I still get excited when I see famous people and erm I . . . I, still get overcome with a tremendous desire to say, 'Oh, you're . . . Oh.' (*laughter*) and erm . . . and I work in a cinema, and a lot of famous people come into the cinema, and it's very . . . strange to sort of sell tickets to erm . . . Bryan Ferry or, as it was the other day, to Ray Davies of the Kinks (*laughter*) and that was a big moment for me because I think he's great and I love his songs and his music and I so badly wanted to say to him,'Oh, Ray, I love your music' and I was just too shy to . . . you know . . . I just couldn't do it and instead, you know, I, I we talked about the film which I didn't like very much and I was kind of trying to be you know terribly witty and clever with him and he was just such a kind of . . . he was a really regular guy really . . . a bit odd I mean slightly sort of quirky, but erm just you know . . . really quite sort of normal and sweet and erm I never did tell him how much I enjoyed Waterloo Sunset. (*Oh . . .*)

9B He had this shock of electricity type hair

EXERCISE 2

Well certainly the experience that I had, I was about sixteen or seventeen at the time and I was into guitar music. I loved playing electric guitar music and my younger brother took me along to see a certain musician play and I knew all these guitar phrases in my head and the first one that sent me was . . . (*guitar sounds*) and he said, 'We're going to see Jimi.' And I said, 'It's not believable we're going to see Jimi – Jimi who?' and he said, 'Jimi Hendrix' and it was at the Marquee Club and I was seventeen years of age and I said I must meet the man and he played a gig that night where I was just sent to heaven and back for the price of seventeen and sixpence to get into this club. And I went up to him and I forced myself into his little room and I met this man who was only five foot seven and a half, and I was six foot two, with this shock of Afro hair because at that time you know, coming from the part of Africa I did, everyone kept their hair short and he had this shock of electricity type hair and I went up to him and I said, 'I must have your autograph', and he went, 'Hey man, OK, fine', you know . . . and he wrote his signature out to me and I said, 'Look Jimi, tell me what is that chord that you're playing in Foxy Lady?' and he went, 'Hey, man . . . I don't play chords, I just play the sounds'. (*laughter*) So I said to him, 'Well, OK, OK, OK. How can I learn to play like you?' and he said, 'Feel it, experience yourself'. So I just remember that experience was meeting Jimi Hendrix and it just sent me to heaven and back and he was . . . he was so giving. He was a musician . . . great person and I still can't get that guitar lick together now. (*laughter*)

EXERCISE 3

One day sitting in what had actually turned out to be an incredibly dreary rehearsal for something so I won't mention what it was . . . erm . . . a chap came through and just sat down in front of me . . . That was a gulp. It was . . . Paul Newman . . . he was just kind of sitting there with this . . . he must be about sixty now but he's in extremely good shape with this just white fluff of hair . . . it was cut in the way it always was and you just wanted to sort of touch it . . . because I've been in love with Paul Newman since I was very small, it's those very bright big blue eyes . . . and when he sort of turned round to me and said, 'Hello . . . ' . . . aagh . . . I went totally tongue-tied, a complete idiot because I couldn't think of two words to say apart from 'erm, hello, how are you?' (*oh . . .*) . . . that was basically it. I was a complete and absolute dopey because I wasn't expecting it . . . and there he was looking beautiful, dapper, big blue-eyed, just a hint of very adorable tan on the face, you know just that bit and I became the total fan . . . the total . . . I didn't come out with, 'Can I have your autograph, please?' 'cause I couldn't get the words out of my mouth. But I actually stayed and I could have left . . . I actually stayed for the next hour and a half just gazing on this chap or trying to read . . . I don't really care that Paul Newman's in the room . . . aagh . . . from behind a newspaper . . . sorry, but he is rather gorgeous (*laughter*) and he's not five foot two. There was this thing about him being five foot two . . . he's a good five ten . . . and he wasn't wearing stacked heels, because I looked. (*laughter*)

Unit 10 The hole

10B The hole

EXERCISES 1, 2, 3 AND 4

There was a river with a small town either side of it. They were linked by a road that ran across a bridge.

One day, a hole appeared in the bridge. Both towns agreed that the hole should be mended. However, disagreement arose as to who should mend it. Each town considered itself superior to the other. The town on the right bank claimed that it was the principal destination of the road, so the left-bank town, being of less consequence, should mend the hole. The town on the left bank, on the other hand, maintained that all the traffic came to them, so it was in the interest of the right-bank town to mend the bridge.

The dispute went on, and so did the hole. The more it went on, the more the hostility between the two towns grew.
(*music*)

One day a local tramp fell into the hole and

broke his leg. People from both towns questioned him closely about whether he was walking from the right bank to the left, or from the left bank to the right, in order to decide which town was responsible for the accident. But he could not remember, since he was drunk that night.
(*music*)

Some time later, a coach was crossing the bridge. It fell into the hole, and broke an axle. Neither town took any notice of the accident, as the traveller was not going from one to the other, but was merely passing through. The angry traveller got out and asked why the hole had not been mended.

On hearing the reason, he declared, 'I shall buy this hole. Who is the owner?'

Both towns at once declared that they owned the hole.

'One or the other, whoever owns the hole must prove it.'

'How shall we prove it?' asked both sides.

'That's simple. Only the owner of the hole has the right to mend it. I shall buy the hole from whoever mends the bridge.'

The people from both towns rushed to do the job while the traveller smoked a cigar and his coachman changed the axle. They mended the bridge in no time, and asked for the money for the hole.

'What hole?' The traveller looked surprised. 'I can't see any hole. I've been looking for a decent hole for some time now. I'm prepared to pay a good price for it, but there's no hole here. Are you pulling my leg or what?'

He got into his carriage and drove off.
(*music*)

The people of the two small towns have now become reconciled. Now they lie in wait on the bridge in perfect harmony, and whenever a traveller comes along they stop him and beat him up.

10C Reaction

EXERCISE 1

– Well, after listening very closely to this story, I couldn't understand why it ended up on a rather violent note, such as beat him up. Er, I'm not in agreement with that. Er, I was interested with the story, I was interested with the plight of the various people in it but violence to me always negates the purpose of a story. I'm sorry to say, it's a negative, er, note. But I stand by my word.
– Well I thought, I thought it was quite amusing, actually. I, I, erm, I, I rather admired the, the, the er wily traveller who managed to er get what he wanted by erm, by such devious means and er, I mean it's a little sort of morality tale I suppose. I don't know how true it would be, I mean er, it, it rather suggests that the villagers are simpletons and that that the person passing through is, you know is, is is far cleverer than them and nobody was able to see what was going on but erm, yes, it was, it was quite a funny little story.
– I can quite believe the self-interest of, of each village in not wanting to lift a finger unless it affected them in some way. But usually with these stories there's a, there is a moral at the end and this one there wasn't . . . I mean, you're right, the violence, you know, it's not, er, it's not a very nice er thing to end on I don't think.
– Yes, when I was reading it, I hadn't read it before and I was interested to see how it would end. And I must say that the fact that he got the hole filled in, by his own devious means was really funny but then, I don't know why they're beating up the travellers. I mean, obviously, they got it in for that one particular one but I didn't really understand the moral . . . as to why they beat up all the travellers.

Unit 11 Teeth and dentists

11A Childhood memories

EXERCISE 2

– When I was a child, my teeth used to point in several different directions and, er, inevitably that involved some complicated and I think rather expensive, er, dentistry. And, and, my sort of horrible memory is of wearing lots of wire bands, around my teeth for years and years. Didn't really do much good because they're, they seem to be sliding back into their positions now.
– Well my teeth, er, when I was a child were . . . appalling. Er, where I come from, which is Scotland, has got, the er, worst rate of er, dentistry in Great Britain. Because in Scotland we tend to eat a great deal of sugar . . . Er, also we tend to eat a lot of fried

food in Scotland, which of course is not very good for the gums. So when I was about fourteen, I had false teeth, which is, er, terrible for a young boy of fourteen.

– Well I, as a child, never imagined that I would have problems with my teeth, er, but I, I did. It wasn't something that was conscious to me at the time, it was something that as I developed I realised that I had two very prominent front teeth which protruded and stuck out. Er, and, and like some of us round the table had to have considerable work done on them to straighten these teeth out.

EXERCISE 3

– I realised that I had two very prominent front teeth which protruded and stuck out. Er, and, and like some of us round the table had to have considerable work done on them to straighten these teeth out. Er, it meant several visits to dentists to have mouldings made of my teeth and I used to like that because they used to use a, a substance, a sort of like a, it was like sort of a chalky substance which they used to take an impression of the teeth, and I loved that, because it tasted of peppermint. And every time I knew I was going to have one of these sort of impressions made, I used to just relish the thought and couldn't wait to get to the dentist. But that must be one of the few occasions when I, I actually enjoyed going to the dentist.
– They didn't have that in, in Scotland. What they did was they . . . it was like window putty. (*laughter . . . that's right*) It was the most disgusting thing I've ever tasted.
– Is that that sort of it almost ends up like jelly . . .
– That's right. And it explodes in your mouth.
– Gosh, I never had that.
– Did you find that kids made fun of you when you were wearing braces, teeth braces?
– Well I used to, er, no I actually used it to advantage. At one stage I had some very dramatic braces which were top and bottom stuck together and I was really only supposed to wear them at night. (*right*) But to show off, which I used to do rather a lot, I used to wear them to school in the day and told the teacher that I had to wear them all the time (*laughter*) so I couldn't talk at all because my jaws were stuck together like this.
– I think that's very inventive of you.
– Quite enjoyable.
– To use something that might have been seen as a disadvantage as being the one and only, you know, using it for that. Weren't they terribly uncomfortable?
– Horrible! They hurt, too, because they (*didn't they dig into gums and things?*) they dislocated your jaw, really, they shifted things about, so, (*yes*) it felt, when you took them off it felt like someone had punched you in the jaw or something.

11B Vivid experiences at the dentist's

EXERCISE 3

I'm in fact probably terrified of dentists. But it's the erm, it's the injections, basically. That I cannot stand. I will think of anything. I think of the green fields of Ireland, I think of the Atlantic, I think of anything rather than–you know, my toes turn up, my arms go rigid, my hands, you know, tight, go white at the knuckles and things like that. I think of the worst dentist I ever had and he was the absolute nasty person, at the age of sixteen, he actually took a tooth out for no good reason it seemed to me. Erm, he said it was abscessed. He said, he tapped it with a metal hammer type of thing and I sort of went 'Ouch' and he said, 'Well that's got to come out'. Said, 'It won't hurt'. And not knowing any better, I let him do it. Had a bit of gas and stuff like that and half-way I thought I was being extremely brave, thinking of everything, I was controlling it, I was being you know whatever, and half-way through this awful cracking sound he said, 'Oh, she's a good one, she hasn't thrown up yet'. (*laughter*) At which point I threw up, I passed out, I screamed, and I was in agony.

EXERCISE 4

I've never yet met a poor dentist. (*mm*) It's incredible. They er, and they're always incredibly busy. Er, if you try to get an appointment with a dentist, er, you have to wait three or four weeks. I can never understand that either. It's like doctors – you have to wait three or four weeks to see a doctor. So you've got to be ill for three or four weeks or you've got to have toothache for three or four weeks. But the thing about dentists is that what kind of job is it looking down someone's mouth all the time? You know, it must be a disgusting job. You know, and, and, to, work in that kind of clinical atmosphere all the time must drive you potty. I know one of the biggest suicide rates are dentists. (*really?*) Yes. (*oh*) So it's, er, I can understand it, I wouldn't want to be a dentist.

EXERCISE 5

I had a for a while a Canadian dentist, and she was very, very short. Very short. And the only time I've ever had an extraction, I had this tooth out, and in order to pull it out she had to get on a little box. (*laughter*) She had this special little box and it was terribly disconcerting because I knew it was serious business when I saw her sort of step on this box. And because she was very small it was also a sort of two-handed job and although the, the anaesthetic was quite successful, I have this vivid recollection of this tiny little woman with sort of two fists in my mouth pulling away and stood on this box, it was, well, if I hadn't been crying, I'd have laughed.

Unit 12 Take our advice

12A Learning to drive

EXERCISE 2

(*music*)
With this tape we're going to help you pass your driving test. Use the tape and the booklet at home or in a stationary car but obviously, don't use them when the car is moving. Now if you really want to pass your test, then take some lessons with a qualified driving instructor and use the tape for practice and revision. Use it every time you practise and that will give you a really good chance of passing first time.
(*music*)

EXERCISE 3

Now before we start on the steering wheel, let's have a look at diagram 1 in the booklet. Figure 1 shows the hands in the ten to two position. Just think of a clock face, with your left hand at ten o'clock, and your right hand at two o'clock. Or you could use a quarter to three position. Whichever one you use, make sure your thumbs are on the inside edge of the wheel. There's no need to hang on like grim death; just hold the wheel firmly and confidently. And always keep both hands on the wheel, unless you have to take one off to make an essential driving movement, like changing gear. When you turn the wheel, you're going to use the pull–push method. Figures 2 to 6 show what happens when you're turning right. Figure 2 shows the right hand sliding up to twelve o'clock, gripping the wheel and pulling down to the right. Figure 3 shows the left hand letting the wheel pass freely through it while it slides down to eight o'clock. Now you can see why you need to keep your thumbs along the inside edge of the wheel, so that they don't get caught in the spokes.

12B Starting a business

EXERCISE 2

(*music*)
Presenter 1: Welcome to the sound side of the Lloyd's Bank Business Starter Pack. We're bringing together some of the theories and ideas covered in the leaflets in the pack, from a practical point of view.
Presenter 2: And because an ounce of practice is worth a pound of theory, we've brought together first hand accounts by people like you. We've asked them to describe what it was like for them to start a business. And some of the most important things to look out for.
Presenter 1: For example, What was it like to begin with?
A: In a word, exhilarating. That's what it were.
B: I thought to myself: independence at last. Er . . . that's the way I felt about the whole thing, really.
C: Well, I got myself going and . . . I was glad and a bit worried – together, if you see what I mean.
D: Well once I'd started I kept asking myself, Why did I never do it before?
Presenter 1: They make it sound easy. You want to do it? Then just do it! It's about as hard as making a cup of coffee.
Presenter 2: And almost as instant.
Presenter 1: Right. But of course we were asking our four new business people what they felt like. When we asked them how they got started, what they actually did first, they gave us a different kind of answer.
Presenter 2: Without exception, they told us, First, I had a dream, then I made a plan.
A: I just sat down, I wrote out everything I knew about the business. I mean, there was plenty I didn't know, er . . . even with all

the years in the trade. So I made sure I filled in the gaps before I saw the bank manager.

B: It was like being back at college. Um . . . answer these questions. Except that you had to think of the actual questions as well. Looking back, fourteen months later, I'm, I'm glad I went through it as carefully as I did.

C: Well, my idea started by just talking to friends. I didn't think about planning at first, but by the time I put all my notes together, I realised I'd really written a business plan. Looking back, I would have felt a fool without it.

D: It was my plan that actually helped me discover I'd need a partner, somebody to do things I wouldn't have time for. So then I wrote a new plan to persuade him that I had a good idea.

EXERCISE 3

(*music*)

Presenter 1: You heard Alan's voice on side A. He makes specialist goods and sells them, pretty successfully it seems, to high quality food shops around Yorkshire. What went wrong, Alan?

A: I suppose you could say I was too trusting. Remember I did my market research with questionnaires to the local shops. I turned up quite a few customers that way, and they were all coming back for more. Well, I got busy, a bit behind with the invoicing. Next thing I knew, the bills weren't being paid. Only a couple, mind, but by the time I'd realised what was going on, there were several thousand pounds involved. And all for goods I'd supplied. I mean, you can't take Yorkshire fancies back once they've been eaten.

Presenter 1: You're right. So your customers owed you money, but were they still customers? Did they want to go on ordering?

A: Oh they certainly kept coming back for more, and that made my problem even worse. I suppose you could say they were good customers – at any rate, they were selling my fancies at a fair old lick!

Presenter 1: So how did you resolve the problem?

A: First, I went to my bank. The manager's an understanding sort. He agreed I could stretch my overdraft for a couple of months. And then he gave me a few tips. For example: I persuaded my biggest supplier, the flour people, to give me longer credit terms. Then, I put pressure on the two main troublemakers. Phone calls, recorded delivery letters, it's all time consuming and not very pleasant either. In the end, I had to give one up for lost. Not the money, mind, just the chap. My solicitors hammered him with a letter or two and in the end he paid up.

EXERCISE 4

Presenter 2: What advice would you give someone like Alan, so they can avoid such problems in the first place? After all, businesses often have to give credit.

Presenter 1: Well, there are a number of things you can do. Before agreeing to give credit, explain you're a new business and that you would therefore prefer to deal for cash. Or no more than seven days. You could offer a small discount for fast payment. After all, one per cent off a bill can prove cheaper than spending time chasing your money. If your customer still wants 30 or 60 days, get a bank reference and two trade references. And take them up. Ask up to what level they'd consider so and so a good risk. Always make your credit terms clear: thirty days after delivery, say. And of course, don't make Alan's mistake and delay sending out invoices. That gives the impression you're not in a hurry for your money. It could even make you look less than efficient. Above all, stay in control. Make sure your records tell you at a glance how much money you're owed, and how long it's been owing. You'll soon spot which customers you can trust, and which are proving, in Alan's words, troublemakers.

Unit 13 Emotions

13A Crying

EXERCISE 3

Speaker 1

I cry a lot. I, erm, I, I have a great ability to cry. At, erm, anything, really, I mean you name it; films, erm, er, sad articles in newspapers, – erm, my own life, my, the life of my, my parents, you know, anything, many things make me cry. I think I'm quite an emotional person.

Speaker 2
I mean, because I tend to laugh and express myself easily, because that's part of my culture as a black person, I tend to find that crying and weeping come. And even more so during bereavement.

Speaker 3
I don't know, I mean, I've found I myself . . . as very evenly tempered, I, I would only really cry at a really sad film, that's about it, or the birth of a baby, that was always quite emotional.

EXERCISE 4

Speaker 1
I cry a lot. I, erm, I, I have a great ability to cry. At, erm, anything, really, I mean you name it; films, erm, er, sad articles in newspapers, – erm, my own life, my, the life of my, my parents, you know, anything, many things make me cry. I think I'm quite an emotional person. Erm, I find it an immense relief and er, and I would, and I always feel it would be, the world would be a better place if, if certainly the Western world, or maybe perhaps more specifically Britain . . . Great Britain would be a better place if people did vent their, their, their grief or whatever, and er, er, more openly, more freely. Erm, I remember somebody saying that er, that women live longer because they cry. Now I think men definitely should cry more because it's, erm, we, you know, it's in all of us, we all, we all feel sorrow or whatever and it needs to come out, you know. And I, and I, always feel very happy – this is going to sound awful – I always feel, you know it's, it's a good thing to see a man crying. I think it's, erm, you know it shows that they are actually able to show that side of themselves.

Speaker 2
I mean, because I tend to laugh and express myself easily, because that's part of my culture as a black person, I tend to find that crying and weeping come. And even more so during bereavement. I remember when my father died. A very very important thing was to see mourners who weeped, who sort of wept over every possible occasion, and some of them were paid. (*laughter*) Because they made it into a national anthem to weep and to cry and show your emotions to, to allow every feeling of joy and happiness that you had for that man be flooded into tears in order to rid yourself of the spirit of bereavement. And if you don't 'bereave' deeply enough, you carry on your feelings for that person or that man. So I think it's really important to let it out.

Speaker 3
I don't know, I mean, I've found I myself . . . as very evenly tempered, I, I would only really cry at a really sad film, that's about it, or the birth of a baby, that was always quite emotional. Until I, I actually did counselling training and then I realised how bad . . . it is to keep any emotions, whether it's sadness, anger, happiness, to keep anything in is so destructive as you said, and when you do counselling training you, you're forced to kind of be counselled yourself so you have to find, you've got to find something to talk about, obviously, when people are asking you questions. And you, you delve deep down and I found out all sorts of things that I had kind of hidden away, really, you know? I thought they weren't important and, but and when you bring them out, they've gone then, and they're cleared, and you can start with a clean slate.

13B Anger and how to deal with it

EXERCISE 2

– I think the whole spirit also of, of sort of repressed emotions is particulary strong in, in London. And particularly strong as well in cars, in traffic. I notice when I'm driving around the amount of repressed anger (*mm*) that, that exists on the roads, you can just, you know, if somebody if, if for some reason you know the traffic, somebody's waiting at the traffic lights, the traffic lights turn green and that person doesn't move, you can feel, everybody is sitting in their cars just waiting, you know, just slamming on the horn and, and you know, move along, and I notice it myself when I'm driving, is that you know you're in a sort of a closed little container where, where you, you can emote as much as you like because you're not actually having to to deal with it realistically, you know, And I get so angry when I'm in my car, you know, I could kill.
– Well that's why I will always say to you: ride a bike. (*laughter*)

EXERCISE 3

Speaker 1
I actually . . . I, I very rarely get angry, erm, I, I've quite a long tether when it comes to anger, erm, which doesn't mean, I really don't believe I'm suppressing any anger at all, er, but, it manifests itself in a very sarcastic way with me. Like if for example, I'm I'm, if I'm buying a . . . railway ticket or something and the, . . . the guy behind the counter is very surly and er, you know refuses to treat me, er like a human being, I won't be, get angry with him but I'll get very sarcastic with him and try to make very very clever remarks (*oh . . . yes, one of those, yes . . .*) (*laughter*). And er that for me, that for me serves its purpose. I do feel er very . . . I feel very cleansed after a situation like that. Oh, I, of course I do sometimes, if it's absolutely necessary I do get very angry, if I'm taken that far. But I certainly don't suppress any anger.

Speaker 2
Well my anger is tied up with my sleepless nights. (*laughter*) I mean, if I do not sleep well, I wake up the morning, I am angry. I use any excuse to vent my anger on anybody. If I sleep well, then everything's fine. I'm a joyous, warm, loving person. Sleepless nights, I'm full of anger and my anger does not ebb away unless I use a thing or somebody to vent it upon. As weak as that may sound, that's how I work. (*mm*) And it's a terrible sort of admission to make to everybody here. (*laughter*)

– How does your wife cope?
– She doesn't. She doesn't. Er, we, we have lots of angry, er . . . 'cause she's a very volatile person, she's French. So she tends to emote a lot and she uses her anger in the same way that I use my anger. If I'm looking for excuses for having woken up in a particularly bad way, so, er . . . in a way, anger is something that I have to get out. I do not carry it around by weeping, and like crying. I believe in dumping it.

EXERCISE 5

– Apparently, in, er . . . I don't know if this is true, but in Japan, er, if factory workers er get a bit uptight or angry, they can go out into er, the gym or something which is usually attached to the factory and there are punch bags there with pictures of their boss. (*laughter*) And they can go and they can spend twenty minutes punching hell out of this punch bag. (*great . . . oh right*) And they go back to work and they feel great.
– Oh God yes, well, that brings us on to laughing then. (*laughter*) That made me laugh.
– Well that's one way of dealing with anger as well, I suppose, if you can actually remove yourself from the situation and just laugh at it. Um, I think laughter is, is again, one of the most wonderful releases, and, and, er I mean I think that it's actually been proved that you know the chemical that is released when you laugh is, is is life-enhancing and life, er elongating too, you know (*yeah*). It promotes a healthy, a healthier being.
– And it heals wounds . . .

Unit 14 Flirting with danger

14A We've had some near misses . . .

EXERCISE 2

– What kind of equipment do you need for caving? What would you say you need to start caving?
– Money. (*no*)
– You don't need much money. You need warm clothes. You need specialist warm clothes that are light and strong (*mm*) because the clothing especially, everything but especially the clothing takes a lot of wear, erm . . .
– It should be warm when it's wet.
– Something to keep the water off. A waterproof suit.
– A light.
– And a helmet.
– And a helmet. Wellie boots.
– And some people to go with.
– And do you need ropes, and . . .
– No, not to start with. (*mm*) Lots of caves you can go in without doing any of this dangling above vast drops business. (*mm*)
– But for European caving, yes, you need an awful lot of rope. (*mm.*) Um, we, when we go to Spain we take something like a kilometre (*or more*). Two, two . . .
– More like three . . .
– Two kilometres of rope with us, taking an average. So, yes, you need that. And personally, you need equipment for getting up and down the rope. You need a device for sliding down the rope with enough friction to

stop you hitting the bottom. And you need at least two jammer . . . jamming devices to . . . so that you can get up the rope without sliding down it again. That's basically all you need.

EXERCISE 3

– Do you ever think about the danger? Don't you think it's dangerous?
– Yes.
– Yes. So what? (*laughter*)
– I don't think it's dangerous.
– It's not dangerous compared to say playing rugby football.
– Yeah, the number of people you know who have actually . . . who are walking round with pins in their joints from playing rugby and having their shoulders ripped apart. I mean, I don't know any caver who has had his shoulder ripped apart. I know one with a wooden leg or something like that but he was run over by a tram . . . he didn't do it caving.
– Oh, he told me it was a bus. He said it was a number nine bus. And he said, the moral of the story is, he said to me, there's no double-decker buses down caves.
– I don't think you think very much about danger when you're in the cave.
– Well, some of the time you do. (*mm*) I find I still have times when I get irrationally frightened . . . where it's perhaps somewhere I've been lots of times and I know it well, and for some reason on a particular day, you're nervous and you don't know why.
– When people ask you what's awful about caving, they think about people being stuck in things. I think that's always . . . the thing that's always frightened me is the fact that really, a lot of the time you're just hung by not very much over an awfully big black hole.
– What, like in 'Just awesome'? Now that is the ultimate big black hole.
– Yeah.
– But it's safe, though . . .
– It's safe? What do you mean it's safe? You know, I don't know who put that bolt in but it's about half way up the rock, you know, you're hanging there with forty metres of absolutely nothing . . .
– It's safe.
– . . . with a waterfall running down by your left shoulder, and if you look at the thing you're hanging off, well it's this piece of steel sticking out of the rock . . . and there's this bloody great crack running down the rock towards it, and . . . it doesn't really feel very safe.
– It's safe in terms of, it's unlikely that you're going to have an accident. But the consequences of having anything other than a very small accident are quite . . . potentially severe.

EXERCISE 4

– We've certainly found that the times when we've had even small accidents in caves, like remember when Fred had that stone kicked on to his face . . . and it was really lucky he was quite near the entrance, otherwise he would have had a hell of a time getting out. (*And he's a very strong person.*) It was something that was easily fixable when we got him to hospital, it was just the distance of . . . (*mm*) getting him out of the cave, spending a night at top camp being looked after by the medics, getting him down the hill in the morning, putting him in the car, driving to Oviedo . . .
– But have you had lots of accidents, I mean have . . .
– We've had some near misses. I mean, there have been occasions when there has actually been objective danger.
– What? Objective danger, what does that mean?
– In Gavin's case, when he was down in the boulder choke (*oh, yeah*) he was lying there, heard this rumbling so he shuffled back a little bit and this boulder fell where his head had just been. That is real danger. (*yeah*)
– Well yes, but I mean, it didn't fall on his head, did it? (*laughter*)
– No. He survived. It was a near miss. We've been fortunate in that we haven't had any serious accidents. (*mmmm*)

14B It's not inherently dangerous but . . .

EXERCISE 1

– Frank, how long have you been a glider pilot?
– I've been gliding for the past ten years. I've actually been flying since I was a teenager but I got into gliding as a sport about ten years ago.
– How long does it take to train to fly on your own in a glider . . . usually?

– Usually . . . erm . . . the average is about er sixteen hours, for 42 take-offs and landings, some do it quicker.
– Uh huh, how big is an average glider?
– Erm . . . these days they tend to go to about eighteen metres for the single seaters. The basic trainers are nineteen or twenty-metre wingspan.
– Right, and they're made of fibre glass these days?
– These days fibre glass, in particular for about the past fifteen to twenty years, it gives a much more efficient wing shape.
– Now if I wanted to go on a first training flight, erm where would I sit in the glider?
– Commonly the front seat, there are very few side-by-side trainers. In gliding you're seated in tandem with the instructor in the rear seat.
– So the trainee sits in the front?
– That's correct.

EXERCISES 2 AND 3

– And how much room is there inside a glider? Is it comfortable?
– Oh more than your average 727 seat. There's much more elbow room. They appear to be narrow, but in fact it's like a big armchair in the sky.
– Can you turn round to speak to the pilot if you're sitting in the front?
– Oh, you can turn your head but it's like anybody else sitting about a metre behind you. There's no difficulty in talking, er, you don't have to use an intercom, you just use a normal voice and there's only the sound of the air passing over the canopy, and it's not particularly loud.
– So do some people who go up for the first time like to have the pilot talking to them regularly just to make sure he's not asleep?
– Ah, yes . . . funny you should mention that because that's happened to me once when I had a friend up and we'd been chatting a bit and then we were finally in the circuit to land and I'd been quiet the last couple of minutes basically just to let him look about and er enjoy the experience and I suddenly spoke again and he jumped and suddenly became aware that he'd missed my voice for the last couple of minutes, so generally if I'm going to go quiet I tell my passengers now I'm just going to let them enjoy the flight and if they have any questions to ask they may and erm, I, I, just avoid that feeling that perhaps you're all alone up there, and there's somebody not behind you any more.
– What sort of sensations do you get up in a glider when you're in the sky there?
– Erm, it's not like standing on the edge of a building or a cliff but it's a like standing or sitting I should say on a comfortable chair on a scenic look-out er and one tends to look out not immediately down ah and the sensations are of course that there is movement ah but it's for the most part ah pretty gentle . . .
– Is there a legal retirement age for gliding, or do people just glide on into the sky and off into the great beyond?
– I don't think so, er . . . we have an instructor who's well into his seventies now and flying regularly (*an instructor?*) yes, we have had several people who in their sixties have retired and then learnt to fly, and matter of fact I know of a chap who's over ninety now well that you mention who flies his own home-built aircraft up at Kapunda, it's got a little Volkswagen motor in it.
– Over ninety?
– Mm, as long as you can pass a medical, I can't see that there's any reason why you shouldn't.
– Why, why does gliding appeal to you, why have you come to love it?
– Oh, it's the classic getting away from it all, erm it's almost like painting – it forces your mind off everything else, you must concentrate on what you're doing, erm it's not inherently dangerous er to use a quote but like the sea, it's unforgiving of any incapacity or carelessness or neglect.
– Well, thanks very much for talking to me. That's a very interesting insight. Thanks.
– You're welcome.

Unit 15 Feet and walking

15A My poor feet

EXERCISE 2

Speaker 1

I have what are called Piscean feet because I'm a Pisces and that actually means that we weren't intended to have feet, consequently every single pair of shoes I buy for the first . . . month, sometimes six weeks are absolute agony. I can buy shoes that are slightly too big in order to make them feel comfortable I think but that never works either, they'll get me in the end and erm my . . . my poor feet seem to suffer so much.

Speaker 2
People say I'm very primitive because I can pick things up with my feet and I tend to open doors with my feet (*laughter*) and knock things over with my feet but I also have a problem, because my feet are very small and like you I suffer when I buy a pair of shoes. I can get them small, I can get them big, but they always hurt until the shoe becomes really old and rather disgusting to look at, I'm not comfortable, and I look at other people with envy . . . these beautiful high heels, lovely boots and of course I can't wear them because my feet are too small.

Speaker 3
Well, I you may have noticed have on a pair of cowboy boots today and I suppose that's a concession to my home state or something but er no I tend to go for er very comfortable shoes because I years ago had a terrible problem with my feet, I . . . this was about six or seven years ago when I started dancing and er I started doing modern dance classes and got into a modern company and er found that dancing on different surfaces, some surfaces would actually rip the skin off the bottom of my feet and er it was just it was terrible but that's when I started wearing very comfortable shoes I suppose.

EXERCISES 3 AND 4

The area of feet that fascinates me is the actual . . . other people touching your feet . . . you know we very rarely let people do that, not only in the privacy of our own homes . . . and it's part of exercises in trust and relaxation and I find it absolutely wonderful to sometimes it's a part of a yoga class or something. You will do some manipulation of the feet and this idea of pressure points in the feet just the act of some . . . when, you know, you're clean and washed (*laughter*) erm I find that area of feet, the social thing of it seems to be a particularly type of, remarkable though it is, naked experience to have someone else touch your feet even though they are the most utilitarian part of the body you could possibly wish to get er and the most public . . . easily accessible they're in fact very rarely touched by anybody and when they are, and you release a lot of the tensions that are hidden in the feet it actually does affect the whole sense of your whole body . . . it's quite remarkable.

15B Two walking stories

EXERCISE 1

I've studied in France and I lived with a very wealthy family and er they were very very kind to me and put up with er all the courses and things that I was going to, and it was customary for students such as myself to usually be loaned a *vélo*, a little motorbike (*mm*) to get about and it was a very hilly area and I had, I didn't have the *vélo*, and I consequently had these terrible blisters and erm I can remember complaining and complaining to the family, 'I think I'll have to do something about my feet, everybody else has got *vélos* to get to college and I, I need a *vélo*' and 'Oh, poor girl' and one day I got home from college and madame said to me, 'Oh, we've got something for your feet Karen' and I thought, at last a *vélo*, a *vélo* for me, and er she said, 'It's in your room'. Now my room was on the first floor (*laughter*) and I thought . . . mm . . . something wrong here, and I went into my room and there was a very large cardboard box with some salts in for hardening the skin (*laughter*) er, some tubes of cream and a lot of elastoplast. (*how sad*) My feet have suffered ever since.

EXERCISE 2

Mm . . . well the longest, er, sort of journey on foot that I've ever attempted was in um it was in Madeira . . . and it was very bold and very foolish . . . erm there's a sort of peak, oh which is called the sort of red peak in the middle of Madeira and it's an eight-hour trek up . . . and er . . . we sort of boo . . . decided to go . . . and er it turned out it was the a footpath which was about sort of six inches wide and sheer drops. I mean the footpath was very neatly carved but sometimes you would be seeing down thousands and thousands of feet, one of the most terrifying things, and of course that that sort of started halfway up the mountain so you you just had to go on or you had to do the same thing the way down . . . and er we did this and the . . . during the night I had the most frightening falling dreams after . . . this eight-hour walk sort of hurtling through space all night and this sort of terrible terrible dreams about falling down precipices . . . and then, when we woke up the next morning we we spent the night in this mountain hut . . . it . . . we, we went out of the door and there was just white, the fog was so thick that you couldn't see six inches in front of your nose and so we sort of felt our way down this mountain . . . it was one of the most frightening experiences but apart from that I'm not much of a walker . . .

Unit 16 Credit cards

16A I use mine for . . .

EXERCISE 2

Speaker 1
But, er, now , now I have one, I have one credit card now. Which is, you know I don't really like it but it's nice to . . . Well like if you book airline tickets . . .

Speaker 2
And so I have a credit card which I use mostly for petrol, I've got another one which I use if I need to get cash in a hurry but otherwise I actually don't use my credit cards very much. What I find useful is I have actually let people into their homes when they've got themselves locked out by using a credit card.

Speaker 3
And also I use it as a statement, a way of getting all the statements done at the end of the month. Because being schedule D tax payer, you have to do all your own tax, (*right*) all right, I can give my accountant a printed tax thing.

EXERCISE 4

– I have to say I absolutely adore credit cards. (*laughter*) But I have had . . . I keep great check on myself and have to watch that everything gets cleared and I don't build up to great heights.
– Do you always pay it off at the end of the month?
– I've got several that I pay off at the end of the month and others that I stagger . . .
– That you don't. Oh, see, that's when it gets dangerous, I think.
– Yes. I stagger. But they're watched, they're watched . . .
– Well, I have credit cards but I actually use a credit card only for petrol and make sure I pay off. I'm very square in that respect, it's because I never handled money as a child. And I'm very erm, wary of spending more than I have. (*mm*) I feel if I've got the money I'll spend it, but if I haven't I just don't want to spend it. And so I have a credit card which I use mostly for petrol, I've got another one which I use if I need to get cash in a hurry but otherwise I actually don't use my credit cards very much. I pay for everything by cheque, more than credit card.

16B Anecdotes about credit cards

EXERCISE 2

– I'll tell you about one awful experience that happened to me, erm, I took out, erm . . . one of these card insurances that cover all your cards (*mm*) should your cards be stolen and I had my handbag snatched in a store and immediately got the store security, who were very quick, got me into their office and we phoned all of the credit cards that I had on me, within ten . . .
– Which is what they tell you to do?
– Yeah. When, I suppose by the time we'd got to all of them it was about half an hour after the bag had been snatched. Got up to the top floor of the office, started ringing round, and the whole thing was done within half an hour. Erm, when the bag was snatched it went through apparently a chain of people, out of the store, and it went two miles away and they managed to . . . three different people had spent over £2,000 on four of my cards . . .
– But you're only liable for the first 50.
– I wasn't liable for any of it. Because thank goodness I had this insurance.
– None of it. Yeah.
– But . . .
– Touch wood quick. That was . . .
– . . . They'd spent it within twenty minutes of stealing.
– That's incredible, isn't it?
– And the thing that absolutely horrified me was I was close to limits on two of the cards, the ones that I do clear every month (*mm, mm*) I was close to the limit I'm allowed on those, and they, both of those cards they went into banks, said they were me, and got (*no!*) well over what the top limit would have been.
– Really! Well it just goes to show, you could walk into a bank and get more than you could possibly ever pay off!
– I couldn't probably, because I go in, and they say, 'No, you've spent it all already!'
– Right, right.

EXERCISE 3

– I recently touring around America found there was a chap I was with . . . He . . . we were booked in by an American organisation into a hotel, paid for by them, but they would not let him go through the lobby to his room unless they had a credit card number to prove that he was a human being that was trustworthy. (*right, right*) In other words we've got to the stage now with credit cards, however friendly you look however wealthy you look or however nice you look . . . (*That's right, it doesn't matter, they just want to see that number*) Excuse me, where is your credit card?
– Because you know you can't rent a major automobile in the States, you know, you can't rent without, without using a credit card, you can't, you know like you were saying go into a hotel . . .
– I think that what's underneath that is the society in which you're only good if you have numbers attached to you, (*mm*) that are computerised, (*yeah*) and can trace you, and everybody's insured against everybody else (*yeah*) and . . . that side of credit I find rather upsetting.
– It's kind of ugly, isn't it?
– Like a lot of people, it's a great facility, if you're disciplined with it.

Unit 17 Friends and friendship

17A I value it above everything else

EXERCISE 2

I think that . . . erm friendship is a unique er . . . chemistry that happens between two people . . . and a lot of people say they've got best friends or my best chum but I actually wonder how many people actually do have a best friend in the real sense of the word. I have two best friends . . . one works in the theatre, and . . . er . . . one is a sort of entrepreneur and we see each other about three or four times a year . . . but I wouldn't call that being a best friend, that is a close friend . . . I think my best friend, without getting too soppy is my wife. She is my total best friend . . . I can discuss anything with her and she can pick up on feelings that I've got inside me whereas my two best chums can never do that unless I'm showing an expression on my face. If I'm showing an expression on my face then they'll say, 'Oh, what's the matter, Campbell?', but . . . er . . . my wife, I can walk into a room and she knows exactly what kind of mood I'm in and that is a best friend.

EXERCISE 3

Speaker 1

. . . erm I also feel that friendship and and this thing about best friends is really someone that can understand you and I, I've I've kept in touch with four . . . no, three people from schooldays and and we, we don't see each other very often er . . . one or two I see perhaps once a year . . . but the thing about it is when we do see each other it's as if there's been no time spent apart and we're able just to slip into our relationship and a kind of feeling that we, we've always had . . . a comfort . . . it's like wearing a pair of shoes that you've had for a long time, it's comfortable, it's safe and it's warm and it's easy and I and I rate friendship . . . a friend as someone who can understand me . . . understand all the nuances and all the facets that I have about me and that I can . . . perform towards them in the same manner.

Speaker 2

I mean I've had friends since childhood and we, we're essential to each other . . . we reflect . . . we reflect erm each other's journey through life and the the changes that we've gone through . . . I think I think there's a difference with men and women. I think sometimes for some women friendship is easier, I think often friendship between men is difficult just because it does happen that men are less used to expressing their emotions, I think the sort of you start off as a as a young girl and a teenager erm making confidences and you don't have that erm . . . so much front to keep up you you confide your failures it's much harder I think sometimes for men to confide their failures and I think a lot of a lot of the trust and the sort of intimacy between women is to do with insecurities and all those things that you share . . . I've felt immensely privileged actually to have a number of very close friends and . . . no . . . I for me it's in terms of human relationships I think I value it above everything.

17B Losing and keeping friends

EXERCISE 1

It's . . . it's maybe very sad to say lose a friend you realise that perhaps you've got nothing else in common it might be after ten years . . . I broke up with my bestest friend, my bestest school friend whose name was also Maggie, in fact there were three of us Maggies one two and three, erm she'd . . . we broke up . . . we actually broke up when she hadn't she hadn't decided she could never decide what she wanted to do and I'd decided what I'd wanted to do and I'd gone on and I was doing it and she wanted it, for some reason this came into it a weird jealousy came into the relationship because she wanted what I . . . I had, she wanted the boyfriend I had, she wanted the career that I was starting . . . and this and it was very very very difficult to contain it and it really got out . . . I was very very sad when it broke up but she was then this friendship that we'd had since we were four or five had then become destructive by the time I was 20 I think I was about 22 at the time 20, I'd just left college and that and that was really disturbing to my even to my . . . I still ring her mother up every now and again to see how she is and she's never settled in all this time she's never actually settled to any particular thing it's one you know, one career and then she starts another, and then she changes and then she might travel for a bit and that sort of thing but it actually became destructive . . .

EXERCISE 2

– But as you were saying about you don't see friends for a long while and then you meet them and you just slide in together . . . there's a I think that happens because of that wonderful word 'trust', 'cause you can trust that you're not going to be laughed at, you can trust that anything you say is going to be in confidence and I mean that's what friendship is, isn't it?
– And it's about making making mistakes and failing because we did all that when we were younger and we've seen each other's foibles (*yeah*) and we know them, but we still like each other. (*yeah*)
– I mean nobody else apart from your parents sees you go through so many things, you know, and can remember apart from your own memory of life they're they're your other memory, and that's that's sort of I mean you remember each other over years and years I mean I've I've a friend who I had chicken pox with when I was four years old and he and I have so much in common you know that's kind of that's unspoken . . . that is just common knowledge.
– Well I think it's true what you said, Anne, about the fact that you do use friends as a as almost the benchmark to your your own development . . . ah . . . and theirs as well, and it's a continuing sort of journey for both of you.

EXERCISE 3

Song 'You've got a friend'.

Unit 18 Learning languages

18A English, what English?

EXERCISE 2

The main language, and this is going to sound really funny, the main language that I learned was English because I come from Glasgow and I was born on the docksides of Glasgow. And if I was to speak in a Glasgow accent you would not understand a single word that I was saying. So when I went to drama school people laughed at me. I mean they literally laughed when I spoke because they couldn't understand a single word. And there's dialect phrases that you've got to get out of your head. Like, erm, the word 'mines'. Now 'mines' is not a place where miners go and mine things, 'mines' is something belonging to you. Like you say, 'that jacket is mines'. Or you use the word 'but' in the wrong place. You put 'but' at the end of a sentence rather than the middle. Like if someone said to you, 'You're wearing your raincoat' and you'd say, 'It's raining'. You wouldn't say that. You would say, 'It's raining but.' And people used to look at you in a very very strange way. (*laughter*) So when I went to drama school I actually had to learn to speak the Queen's English. And I think I've just about achieved it.

EXERCISE 3

– An Irishman will never use one word where he can use ten. (*laughter*) But you get lovely phrases like, er, which English people don't often understand, like 'Hang on a second, I'll be back in a minute' which is, you know the type of thing. When I go home to Ireland, when I go home to Ireland, 'Oh marvellous, beautiful, it's grand. It's great to see you, when are you going home?' (*laughter*) Which doesn't mean, doesn't mean get lost, go away, it's the way of asking how long are

you staying. As I said, the Irish will use ten words where the English will use one. And it's a very warm, lyrical sound.
– But that's because they're poetic.
– Oh much more poetic, much more poetic . . .
– I mean the Irish and the Scots are very poetic.
– Very poetic. And they've got a sense of humour.
– And they've got a sense of humour.
– A wicked sense of humour.
– But when I came to England I had a very strong Indian accent. Er, I . . . can give an example of, of some of . . . the . . . 'Please can you let me know, I would very much like to have some milk today . . . ' so it was that kind of thing. Er, and I didn't think too much about it but other people, other English kids used to look at me and rather like Campbell, you know, kind of laugh at me. So I thought there's something not quite right here. Anyway I used to, used to pick on certain children in the class, used to do very well, they, they used to get very high marks and something inside me said now what is it they've got that I haven't? And I realised that a lot of these kids could speak what is known as the Queen's English so I made up my mind consciously to change the way I spoke – to change my, my dialect and my accent. Er, for better or for worse. And when I was going through this phase of 'Oh please tell me what . . . ' and then changing it to almost to the way I'm speaking now, people would say to me, 'You're not sounding yourself today. Have you . . . you got a cold? (*laughter*) Erm . . . something . . . Is your voice breaking?' (*laughter*) Er . . . my subjects never improved and I, I, I didn't get very, very high marks like these other kids that could speak very well but, er, people did stop laughing at me so I don't know if that's a good thing or a bad thing. I think . . . it's a bit of both.

18B I just sort of had to pick it up

EXERCISE 2

Speaker 1
I learnt in my life, truthfully, three. English being one of them, so let's talk about the other two. The first one I learnt was in India, which is the place that I was born in . . . er, this is going to sound terribly grand but it wasn't quite like that. Er, I come from a fairly middle class background. I was born with a silver spoon in my mouth. So we had servants on the tea estate where I was born and the language that I learnt first was Nepalese. My parents said that I spoke it incredibly well, far better than they did because I used to play with the servants. At the age of four, I left er that part of the world and went to Calcutta. Nepalese stopped. And I have never spoken it since. I . . . later on in life I tried to learn French and Spanish. Er, I succeeded far more with Spanish because I enjoyed going on holiday to various parts of Spain. Er, but my Spanish is just about, I can get myself a coffee and get myself a bed for the night. Ah, so I think that's relatively useful, but, er, by no means as useful as I'd like it to be. So it's an ongoing process . . .

Speaker 2
I've sort of been quite lucky because I never had to learn a language from a book. Er, because my parents travelled round when I was a child, I was sort of plunged into a strange language and just had to sort of pick it up. Erm, and I started off – 'cause I was born in France – speaking both erm French and English, and then er they lived in, erm, in Germany and in Italy as well so in each case it was a question of necessity . . .

EXERCISE 3

Speaker 1
First language was French at er this private school that I went to. I was about seven I suppose, seven or eight . . . that sort of er was interesting till about eleven and then it got to sheer boredom when one changed schools and became a . . . you had an English teacher, an English teacher teaching you French in what was perceived as a perfect French accent. If you actually heard anyone or spoke to anyone in French then you couldn't erm, you couldn't understand a word they said. Because we had this perfectly pronounced English form of speaking French. (*laughter*) And then someone tried to drum in Latin to me, which I actually enjoyed very much. Very much. I liked Latin. And I did Italian for about, I needed another O Level, I did Italian for three months, with a wonderful teacher who was Italian and taught businessmen. Erm, and she spoke Italian. We spoke from our very first lesson and it was fantastic. And in three months I learned enough to, to erm, to get an O Level with and converse. Unfortunately she was dropped and they came

in with a teacher. A schoolteacher of Italian (*yeah*) who then bored me stupid . . .

Speaker 2
Well, I'm a complete failure. I er, I didn't learn any languages at school. In Scotland it was kind of right down in the curriculum. It was, erm, Scottish schools teach sciences more than they teach anything else. Er, I remember having a French teacher by the name of believe it or not Mr McLoughlin. (*laughter*) How a French teacher got the name of Mr McLoughlin from Aberdeen, I'll never know. So as you can imagine my French was very very poor. In fact, I dropped it in my second year at school. Er, so I haven't learnt any languages . . .

Unit 19A A multicultural world

19A Mixed marriages

EXERCISE 2

- I'm married to a Russian who is naturalised British . . . I had this thing, I never really thought of my husband as Russian. Then I don't think of myself as totally, as British, as being absolutely typical. When I went to the Soviet Union for the first time I tried to imagine him there, and put him into this environment, and I couldn't see him there at all.
- Could I just ask, what did his parents think about you marrying . . . their son?
- They, er, they wanted to know, his mother's a very, very practical Russian lady and she wanted to know everything about me and she was very worried as to what my parents would think about me being with him. Er, that was her greatest concern. And, erm, she couldn't understand, really, couldn't he find a nice Russian girl . . . (*laughter*) that he wanted to be with, and then erm, I was able to go into the Soviet Union and visit and they met me, and gave me the going-over and, er, within a few hours I was in, I knew I was in. They're a very lovely family and they were very very nice to me. And she wasn't troubled by it at all. She couldn't understand, she was very concerned that I, I wouldn't be able to totally understand him, but erm, we . . . she's happy now, especially since she was able to visit, it made a great difference to her.

EXERCISE 3

- But talking about mixed marriages, well my marriage is a mixed one as well. And . . . when my mother-in-law first heard that her son was going to marry a foreigner, and a foreigner who was coloured, (*mm*) she didn't want to know what kind of person I was. All she said was 'Must you really marry someone foreign? Must it really be a foreign person?' And the strange thing is, we've been married a long time and like you we have two children and we don't think of each other as belonging to two different races. And it's only when we're with other people . . .
- Oh, that other people . . .
- Other people . . .
- look at you that way . . . Right
- look at you, and especially the time we got married, which was many, many years ago when there were very few mixed marriages in this country. People used to look at us, and just the look was upsetting. (*mm, yes*)
- Yes. Did your mother-in-law react differently once she'd met you? Did she . . . has she . . . did she change?
- Yes, she changed, she changed a bit. And, she wanted me to be friends. But . . . once she knew me, she didn't think of me as foreign. She said, she sort of said 'Oh well, she's just like everybody else'. And yet, in front of me, if she was watching a television programme there were foreign people, she would always refer to them as foreign. Or if my friends came to visit, or, you know, even people on the street, they were foreign. Because . . . my husband's Scots. And Scots people are very proud of being Scots. And everyone who is not a Scot is a foreigner.

EXERCISE 4

- What I feel about . . . being married to someone from a different country is that you in a way have best of both worlds. You have people from my part of the world coming as visitors and then people from his part of the world coming as visitors and when they meet together – some of them actually have never sort of met foreign people and then they get on famously and think 'Oh well, they're just like us'.'
- If I may say, I think you've put your finger on something terribly important there. As soon as you humanise or personalise that

prejudice, or that basic sort of assumption that person's Sri Lankan or Indian, Jewish, or whatever, as soon as they become personal and you know their name and who they are and how they tick, then suddenly you forget colour and look and all the rest of it. And that's really the, the whole key to I hope what's happening in education with young people and so on . . . It's finding that common humanity. Because then you don't see colour or particular things except as another facet of a fascinating person.

19B Distant relatives

EXERCISE 2

– My family is . . . is really spread all over the world. My father was, er, is a German Jew, my mother's from Holland, and erm, my father came to this country just before the war. And, er . . . my mother came just after the war, and they met actually in England. But, erm, my father's family, in fact both of their families are really scattered from all the way from, a lot of them went to America, erm, a lot of them went to, er Switzerland, erm, some went to Australia, er, some came to, quite a few came to Britain, er some of my mother's family are still in Holland, so, erm, I feel very often that I have relations all over the world, which is actually a really, it's a lovely thing to have, because you can go and visit them, and, erm, I have done, I've seen my American relatives, I've got lots of cousins in, in America.
– Have they all kept in touch, I mean, has your family, obviously they left their country that they'd lived in, but they all kept in contact?
– Yes, yes, there's still a lot of contact between them, erm, my father's family is, is huge, and er, erm, while my grandmother was still alive, there would be regular weekly meetings, erm . . . And, er, every week there would be yet another relation, you know, sort of summoned up from somewhere or other. And, er, and so there's, when I meet them now, which I must admit I don't very often, but recently my cousin got married and there was a big celebration for that, and there they all were, and of course, they all think, they all say to me, 'Oh, do you remember me?' And I remember all of them, you know, they're all really familiar to me. (*laughter*) Erm, and er, they're, it's actually a wonderful thing to have that kind of rich cultural heritage.

EXERCISE 3

– Well my family all live in Texas, all of them, every last one of them. Well, except for one uncle who is a, he works for US Steel, so he's been moving around a lot, but er, they all thought it was very strange that I should want for any reason to leave Texas, let alone the United States, you know, and come over here. And, er, it is strange being so far away from your family, I think because for the first, I think for the first four years I was here I saw them once, very early on, and er, so about three and a half years went by before I saw them again. And, that was very strange, I, I didn't like that much. But it does give them an excuse to come over and visit. My grandmother's over here right now, actually. She's you know this little old lady from Texas and she says, 'Well, I just can't understand people'. And she can't you know. People talk to her and she just doesn't understand. (*laughter*) She just doesn't. And when she's digging round in her purse trying to find the money, you know, and to, she just now, after about four days can tell the difference in a ten and a twenty pound note, so I'm a little worried about leaving her by herself . . . you know, what kind of notes she'll give people . . . remember to get the change, and . . . all of that. And the public transport is completely alien to her. You know, just completely different. 'Cause you know at home she hops in her car and she drives down to wherever she's going and it's just . . . she's not used to the idea of going down an escalator and getting on this train underground . . . and she says she doesn't like that, so I take her on the bus now.
– You wouldn't let her drive here?
– Oh no! (*laughter*) No! God! Imagine the little 74-year-old lady on the wrong side of the road? (*exactly*) With different signs? No, not a chance.

Unit 20 Ngarrindjeri

20A Aboriginal people in Australia

EXERCISE 2

– I know that you've got quite a large family.
– Yes, I've got nine children.

- You've had nine children?
- Nine children.
- And, er . . . or you've got nine children I should say and I've been told you've you have fostered a lot of . . .
- Twenty-three, and today I've got twenty grandchildren.

EXERCISE 3

- My goodness . . . these er these foster children that you had were they immediate relatives, or very distant . . . or closer . . .
- They were close relatives, yes, on my husband's side as well as my side and the longest I've ever had a child, another child for, was four and a half years. But my husband's niece and it was because of a death. A couple of broken marriages . . . I've . . . I also took children in. I felt it was important because home life was very important to us as kids so I just thought it would be better than letting them go to white foster homes . . . Mostly children get fostered . . .

EXERCISE 4

Before the marriages, er, legal marriages by the church, before white man came they was all tribal marriages . . . and a hus . . . a man was allowed to have more than one wife. The Reverend Taplin started the mission off and he was trying to Christianise them so they could learn to become Christians and he, one of the things he did stop was the men having more than one wife, so when William Karpinyeri got converted as they called it in them days, erm, Jane . . . Jane . . . he had to choose between these two women, so he chose the one who had the children as Jane was only a younger girl so, erm, when Jane went back to her family her family felt they . . . he rejected them so they had to turn round and 'mellan' . . . and mellan means kill, er . . . William Karpinyeri's father. Now Taplin wrote that up in his diary and he was very very angry about it but he could . . . there was nothing he could do to stop it and I think that what brought you get these men like Taplin and coming into the mission and trying to change their tribal laws. It must have been a terrible thing for them.

20B Proud to be an Aborigine

EXERCISE 1

I think I've always felt that it was important for us not to isolate ourselves, to get out there and prove that you had capabilities that you could share and bring to the community that you lived in and over the years I think that's been proven . . . er . . . I've done a number of, er, stories with the ABC, storytelling series. I write poetry, er, love music . . . I love young people, and I guess that's my motivation for working at Waryapindi, but underlying all that is the need to retain cultural ties and links. I've always felt that you know Raukkan and the Coorong area is as important to me as Ayers Rock is to people in Central Australia. I have the same deep love of that area . . .

EXERCISE 2

- Is there a chance of you perhaps saying one of your poems, short poems or something like that . . . or is that really putting you . . .
- The one I was thinking of isn't short . . .
- Well how about just say a couple of verses?
- Maybe just a couple of verses of erm . . . 'What it feels like to be black'.

Walking in the sunshine, walking in the shadows
I stare at the concrete columns that hide the blue of the sky
I look at the sea of faces, and not one friendly smile
Where are the camp fires? Where are the stars?
I see only grey buildings standing like guards

I love my old people, I don't love them away
Government departments, just made you a number
They didn't give a damn about sisters and brothers
Aboriginal people are searching to find their way back
Urban Aborigines seeking to find their identities

To the teacher

This book is the third in the *Cambridge Skills for Fluency* series. It follows the formula of the previous two in these ways.

- Each unit is divided into two sections, A and B.
- It encourages learners to employ active listening strategies.
- It encourages learners to make use of what they know of a theme both before and after listening.
- It tries to develop abilities in learners to sample spoken discourse and to extract key information by using the redundancy in conversational English.
- It uses natural spoken English, not scripted material.

In order to build on the abilities developed in the previous books in the series, this book presents additional challenges to learners, who are assumed to be at a good intermediate level. These challenges can be summarised as follows:

- longer and often faster stretches of spoken English
- a greater cross-cultural element (speakers from Africa, Asia, America as well as from Scotland and Ireland)
- more conversations involving several overlapping speakers rather than just monologues (thus producing more complex discourse)
- learners are asked to discuss the themes and their reactions to the speakers more often than in previous books

In one or two units we have also asked learners to think about features of spoken discourse, and to compare English with their own languages. This has enabled us to indicate to learners that their own native language is a valuable comparative resource when building greater awareness of spoken English.

The recordings

All the recordings in the book are unscripted and spontaneous, with the exception of the short story and the authentic guidance cassettes in Unit 12. Many were recorded in a studio and, although some of the speakers do not know each other well, they use a register which reflects a sort of educated informality. Certainly the speakers can be considered good users of the language in the sense that they employ rich vocabularies.

The speakers who are from Africa and Asia do not have strong accents and it is possibly the Scottish accent on the cassette which is the most challenging.

Grading

There is no conscious grading, since with unscripted material on a variety of themes it is not easy to judge what is precisely the basis of difficulty. Within units, however, there are some stretches of listening which are shorter and have a more conventional structure (a story, for example). By studying the themes, tasks and tapescripts, teachers should be able to assess what their particular learners can cope with and make selections and adjustments accordingly. Most units include opportunities for discussion before listening, so teachers can use this phase to pre-teach some vocabulary if that is a form of support they like to give. Generally, we have not pre-empted what those choices of vocabulary items might be.

Using the book

Each unit is divided into two sections, A and B. The sections are linked thematically and can be used either independently or in sequence depending both on time and on the degree of involvement in the themes. Alternatively, segments within sections can be used in conjunction with other materials on the same topic.

Because of the emphasis on spoken response in pairs or groups to the listening material and to the listening tasks, most units assume that classroom interaction is an important motivating accompaniment to listening. Nevertheless, there is plenty of scope for self-study, either at home or in a self-access centre. Students can carry out more detailed listening on their own, either by following the tapescripts or by doing those tasks which were not selected for classroom sessions.

Although we have endeavoured to maintain a gender balance in the recordings, this has not always been possible since the essence of spontaneous language is to allow speakers to select what to say.

Acknowledgements

The authors and publishers are grateful to the following individuals and institutions for permission to reproduce copyright material. It has not been possible to identify the sources of all the material used and in some cases the publishers would welcome information from copyright holders.

p.22 'God save the Queen' arranged by Eleanor Franklin Pike from *The Easiest Tune Books of National Airs, Book 1*, published by Edwin Ashdown, Ltd; p.28 (left) cartoon from *Frustration* by Claire Bretecher, reprinted by permission of Methuen, London and Grove Press Inc., New York; p.28 (right) cartoon from 'Acting One's Age' in *Very Posy* by Posy Simmonds, published by Cape/Arrow, reprinted by permission of the Peters, Fraser & Dunlop Group Ltd; p.48 Ken Taylor for the cartoon; pp.68–9 Ainslie Roberts for drawings published by Art Australia.

For permission to reproduce photographs: p.8 Sally and Richard Greenhill; p.10 Moving Image; p.23 Tessa Sanderson: Andy Clark/Popperfoto; Namibian Independence: John Parkind / Associated Press Ltd; p.24 Timothy Woodcock Photolibrary; p.25 Newcastle Chronicle and Journal Ltd; p.26 (left) English court (scene from the COI film 'A man on trial'): S. Harrison / Camera Press; p.26 (right) court in the former East Germany: dpa/ Zschetzschingck / Camera Press; p.29 Patricia Clarke / 'Fancy That', Wallsend, North Tyneside; p.31 Ben Ross / Camera Press; p.32 (bottom) Jeremy Pembrey; p.34 Nelson Mandela: Jan Kopec, Charles de Gaulle: Leon Herschtritt, Charles Chaplin: Jerome Epstein, Marilyn Monroe: Barron, Kiri Te Kanawa: Jane Brown, Indira Gandhi: Poly/Press, all photographs Camera Press; p.35 Paul Newman: Jerry Watson, Jimi Hendrix: Graham Howe, both Camera Press; p.40 John McCormack, Senior Chief Dental Technician and Brian Hill, Senior Medical Photographer, Newcastle Dental Hospital; p.41 'Toothache' at Wells Cathedral: Woodmamnsterne, dentist with child: Lawrence Migdale / Science Photo Library; p.47 Colin Davey / Camera Press; p.51 (left) J. Allan Cash Ltd; p.51 (right) Paul Brennan in the Culiembro Cave (in the Picos de Europa, Spain): Martin Hicks; p.53 PGL Young Adventure Holidays; p.57 Leslie Garland Picture Library; p.58 Detective Chief Inspector Alan Brown: Roy Letkey; p.66 P.J. Littleton / Camera Press.

For permission to include items on the cassette: Doreen Kartinyeri, Leila Rankine and Dr C. Anderson, Division of Anthropology, Museum of South Australia.

Photographs on pp. 12, 15, 19, 20, 32 (top), 49, 56 and 61 were taken by Jeremy Pembrey.
Drawings by Chris Evans, pp.13, 19, 33, 51, 55, 62; Leslie Marshall, pp.37, 38; Shaun Williams, p.64; Gary Wing, p.10.
Artwork by Peter Ducker, Hardlines and Wenham Arts.
Book designed by Peter Ducker MSTD.